47-600X

LEGENDS OF FLIGHT

BOEING 747

A Legends of Flight Illustrated History

WOLFGANG BORGMANN

SCHIFFER MILITARY
4880 Lower Valley Road Atglen, PA 19310

FSC
www.fsc.org
MIX
Paper from responsible sources
FSC® C104723

Other Schiffer Books by the Author

McDonnell Douglas DC-10/MD-11: A Legends of Flight Illustrated History, ISBN 978-0-7643-6137-1

Boeing 707: A Legends of Flight Illustrated History, ISBN 978-0-7643-6345-0

Boeing 737: A Legends of Flight Illustrated History, ISBN 978-0-7643-6138-8

Other Schiffer Books on Related Subjects

Boeing 757: A Legends of Flight Illustrated History, Dan Dornseif, ISBN 978-0-76436346-7

Originally published as *Die Flugzeugstars: Boeing 747* by Motorbuch Verlag © 2019 Motorbuch Verlag
Translated from the German by David Johnston

Library of Congress Control Number: 2022932549

Cover design by Chris Bower
Type set in DIN/Minion Pro

ISBN: 978-0-7643-6510-2
Printed in China

Published by Schiffer Publishing, Ltd.
4880 Lower Valley Road
Atglen, PA 19310
Phone: (610) 593-1777; Fax: (610) 593-2002
Email: Info@schifferbooks.com
Web: www.schifferbooks.com

CONTENTS

Chapter 6

Fifty years ago, Boeing made aviation history with the 747 program. The crowning achievements of this pioneering work, which was often at a crossroads, were the 747's maiden flight on February 9, 1969, and the awarding of its commercial certification on December 30 of that year. *Rainer Sonntag*

PAN AM
PAN AM

FOREWORD

Welcome aboard the Boeing 747 Huge Viking for a journey through the history of the Jumbo Jet. *SAS*

THE QUEEN OF THE SKY

The Boeing 747 was created as the world's first jumbo jet upon request and with the direct involvement of the board of directors of Pan American World Airways. After the legendary L-049 Constellation of 1939, it was another example of the successful symbiotic form of cooperation between an airline and an aircraft manufacturer in designing a new commercial aircraft. The Connie and the Jumbo Jet have one other thing in common: both were lovingly called "Queens of the Skies" by their fans.

None other than company founder and president Juan Trippe and his technical director John Borger were the driving forces on the airline side, while Joe Sutter, the Boeing factory's leading 747 project engineer, created from the customers' ideas and the internal guidelines of his employer an outstanding design, one that is still unique today, which Boeing patented in the United States in October 1968. The shapes of the 747 are so distinctive that even a layman can immediately identify a "Jumbo." Although the Boeing 747 is in many respects a "Pan American jet," the company avoided

the British aviation industry's mistake made of tailoring excellent designs so strongly to the needs of just one customer that in the end no other airline would have any interest in it. Negative examples of this excessive focusing are the De Havilland / Hawker Siddeley H.S. 121 Trident short- and medium-range jet, developed specially for British European Airways (BEA), and the long-range Vickers VC-10, built for British Overseas Airways Corporation (BOAC). Ironically neither BEA nor BOAC wanted to place the first aircraft designed solely for them into service, since the commercial aviation market had fundamentally changed since the two models were launched.

THE CREATION OF THE JUMBO JET

With the Boeing 747, Joe Sutter and his team succeeded in conceiving a jet whose cabin, initially with nine economy seats per row and two aisles, became the model for all subsequent wide-body jets. Neither Sutter nor the Pan American board of directors had a blueprint that they could have used for orientation. Therefore Juan T. Trippe did not at first think of a wide-body jet for the aircraft with more than four hundred seats that he wanted. He favored a double-decker fuselage with two small fuselage shells, one above the other, and just a single aisle in the upper and lower decks. How a piece of red clothesline was able to convince Juan T. Trippe and John Borger of the alternative and ultimately successful proposal by Joe Sutter can be read in the following detailed history of the 747's development, as can the fact that in 1969 Boeing, with delayed deliveries and resulting low customer numbers, was just able to avoid bankruptcy. The principal cause of the company's financial miseries was the Pratt & Whitney JT9D engine, originally offered as the exclusive power plant for the 747-100. Developed in parallel with the airframe, despite having been certified, the engine was anything but production ready and caused not only Boeing but all early Jumbo Jet customers headaches. Its susceptibility to failures led Lufthansa, among others, to quickly divest itself of its first aircraft and select General Electric as the engine supplier for the more advanced 747-200B. The aircraft's initial teething troubles were not enough, however, to stop the long-term sales success of the Jumbo Jet, which took off primarily thanks to the improved 747-200B and the 747-400, which represented a quantum leap and was developed at the urging of Lufthansa. Ultimately Boeing had no competitors in the over-four-hundred-seat market segment, until the arrival of the Airbus A380. After just Korean Air Lines and Lufthansa placed orders for the passenger version, the actual 747-8 entered service primarily as a freighter and, in a few cases, as a VVIP jet. With its ending production cycle the Jumbo Jet shares the fate of the competing A380, whose last example left the final assembly line at Toulouse, France, in 2021. However, with more than 1,500 aircraft sold since 1965, the 747 is clearly ahead of the A380 by Airbus, which was able to sell only 290 aircraft to fourteen customers. The smaller and more economical long-range twin jets from Seattle and Toulouse have irreversibly replaced the two flying dinosaurs.

Many years will pass, however, before the last 747 is retired and put on display in a museum or is scrapped at an aircraft graveyard. Until then, the large community of Jumbo Jet fans will have the unique opportunity of flying on a 747 or admiring the freighter during takeoff and landing. Gone forever, however, is the "golden age" in which one could comfortably fly to one's destination in big first-class and even economy-class lounges. The Jumbo Jet's upper deck, which after cruising altitude had been reached temporarily became an exquisite restaurant with a breathtaking view from an altitude of 33,000 feet, was legendary. Modern first-class cabins surely offer more personal space and comfort, but the experience of flying in the 1970s was more intense. It was a time in which, despite the beginnings of mass tourism, flying was not yet affordable by all, and passengers—especially in first class—still traveled elegantly dressed. One can still get a small impression of this bygone era of unbroken fascination for the Jumbo jet during a trip back in time to the 1970s in a suburb of Los Angeles. Crew members dressed in historical Pan Am uniforms welcome guests on a virtual

On the occasion of its one hundredth anniversary, British Airways sent its 747-400 jet painted in classic BOAC colors into the air to take part in a formation flight with the Royal Air Force aerobatic team, the Red Arrows. *British Airways*

flight in a 100 percent authentic mockup of the first-class and business-class cabins of a Pan Am 747-121—including the then-legendary cabin service. Pan Am Experience is a place of longing for all those who mourn the demise of what was once the most experienced airline in the world, and the spirit of the times of the 1970s. It was an era in commercial aviation in which the cellular phone and social media had not yet been invented, and one could enjoy a transatlantic flight in relaxation, unreachable by the outside world.

Fasten your seat belts for this literary trip through the fascinating history of the Boeing 747 Jumbo Jet.

Wolfgang Borgmann
Oerlinghausen, summer 2022

Author Wolfgang Borgmann poses in front of the third to last "Jumbo Jet" in the final assembly line at Everett, in June 2022. The 747-8F was built for the US cargo airline Atlas Air. *Ivan Coninx*

The logos of the first customers for the Jumbo Jet adorn the nose of the 747 prototype N7470, which took to the air for the first time on February 9, 1969. *Boeing*

The Scandinavian airline SAS followed the popular trend and in 1967 ordered two 747-200Bs. Delivery was supposed to take place three years later. For the Danish, Norwegian, and Swedish domestic market, with just sixteen million people, the aircraft were, however, far too large. *SAS*

A flight in a Jumbo Jet was and is an experience for all the senses. The almost vertical sidewalls and the ceiling height of 8.3 feet gave the 747 cabin an experience of space unique in commercial aviation. The first-class cabins on the 747 were always the pride of their airlines—as here in a Lufthansa first-class section in 1983. *Siegfried Himmer / Lufthansa*

During the times when the International Air Travel Association (IATA) bindingly fixed air fares for all airlines around the globe, airlines could compete with one another only in terms of the onboard service they offered. This led to the upper decks of 747s being equipped with luxurious first-class lounges until deregulation at the end of the 1970s. *SAS*

Pan Am founder and president Juan Trippe was the driving force behind the development of the Boeing 747. Spurred by a booming air travel market in the mid-1960s, he believed in the need to profitably use even larger jets with more than four hundred seats. However, these optimistic forecasts were not fulfilled, and the twenty-five 747-121s ordered by Pan Am proved difficult to fill and the airline plunged into financial difficulties. *Pan Am*

The silhouette of the 747, with its cockpit enthroned above the main deck, is unique and can be identified as a Jumbo Jet even by aviation laymen.
Wolfgang Borgmann collection

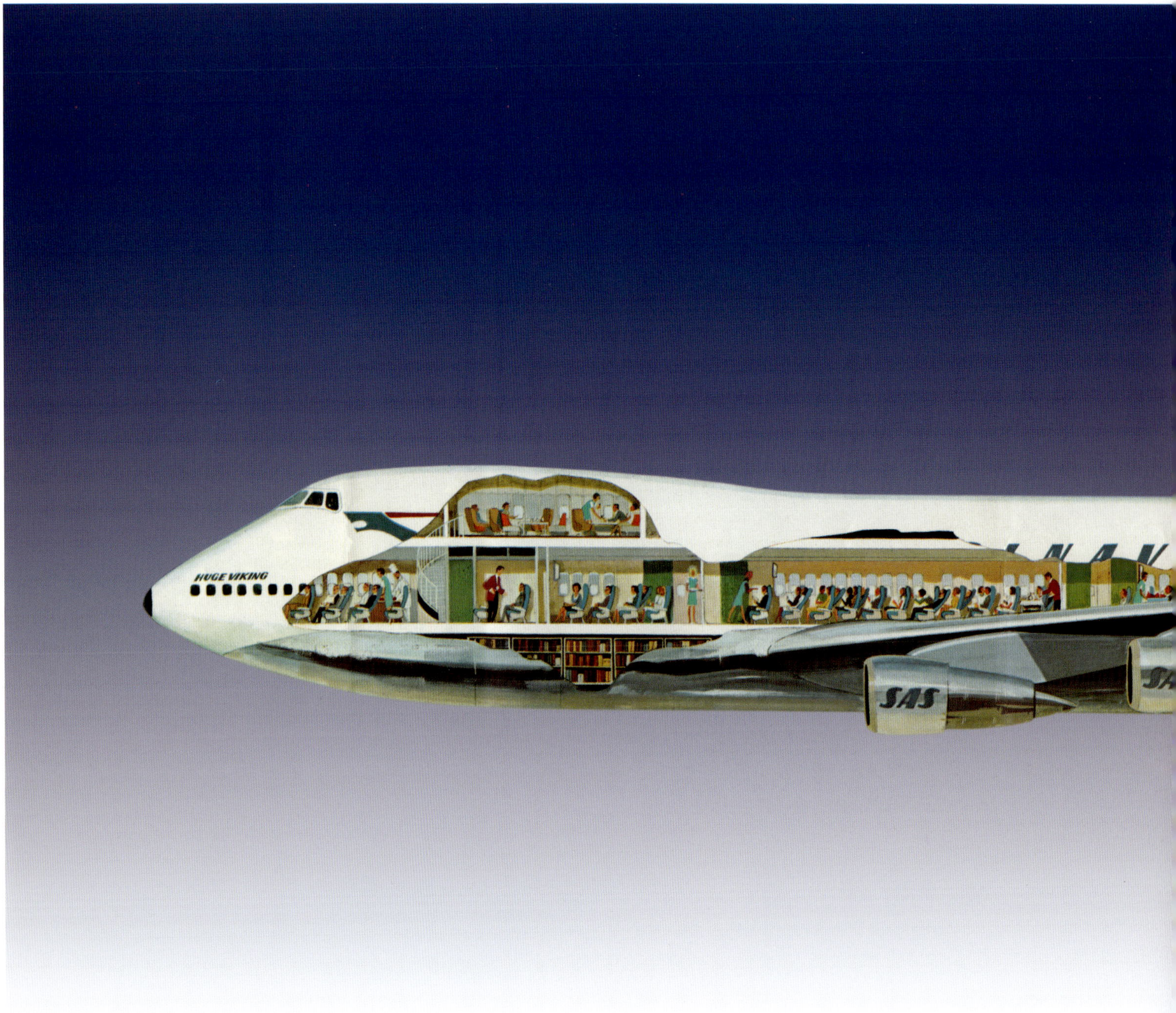

This cutaway drawing shows the breakdown of the cabin of an SAS Boeing 747-200B in the early 1970s. *SAS*

747B
SAS

In the early 1970s the economy-class cabins of most 747 customers were equipped with just nine seats per row and a very generous distance between seats. *SAS*

LIFE

CHAPTER 1
BOEING AND PAN AM

PROJECT BY TWO AVIATION GIANTS

Juan Trippe: "If you build it, I'll buy it."
Bill Allen: "If you buy it, I'll build it."
The informal start of the 747 project during a fishing trip by the presidents of Pan Am and Boeing, Juan Trippe and Bill Allen, in the summer of 1965.

Boeing and Pan Am, that symbiosis between an aircraft maker and an airline unique in the history of aviation, began in the 1930s with luxurious flying boats tailor-made for the network of routes flown by the airline founded in 1927. When Juan Trippe signed the purchase contract for twelve of these Boeing 314 Clippers on July 31, 1936, his Pan American Airways, or PAA, had already begun its steep ascent. After a Fokker F-VII trimotor took off from the muddy strip at Key West on the first flight to Cuba on October 28, 1927, the charismatic company founder's airline expanded unstoppably. In 1928, 1,100 passengers traveled between Cuba and Florida, and a young pilot by the name of Charles Lindbergh, who in 1927 had made headlines worldwide by flying solo from New York to Paris, became one of the young company's first employees. Lindbergh's primary task was that of pathfinder, planning in detail new routes to destinations in the Caribbean and South America in support of his employer's expansion plans. In the pioneering years of aviation there were neither land nor seaplane bases in most Latin American countries, nor were there radio or weather stations. Prior to adding new routes, therefore, PAA had to set these up at its own expense. By the end of 1929, when Trippe made the decision that in the future his airline would cross the oceans and should concentrate on adding new destinations overseas, its route network already covered 14,290 miles and linked twenty-three countries in North and South America. As a first outward sign, PAA became the first airline in the world to dress its aircrews in the navy look, which is still the world standard, with dark-blue trousers and jacket with gold rank

The Lockheed Constellation enabled PAA to become a "global player" in the airline business immediately after the end of the Second World War.
Lockheed Martin

badges on the sleeves plus white shirt and navy-style peaked cap. As usual in Christian seafaring, the two pilots were now called captain and first officer. The aircraft were officially christened with a Clipper name, based on historic merchant ships from American history. Pan Am's legacy thus lived on in the visual appearance of air travel, even after its bankruptcy in 1991.

The first Sikorsky S-40 and S-42 Clipper flying boats were followed by the Martin M-130, designed for PAA. On November 22, 1935, with the maiden flight of NC14716 China Clipper, PAA launched regular air travel over the Pacific. The route taken by the flying boats, which initially carried mail, went from San Francisco to the Philippine capital of Manila with four stops en route, the trip taking a total of seven days. Since flying was done only by day, starting in October 1936 PAA set up comfortable quarters for its passengers on Pacific islands. From them emerged the hotel chain Inter-Continental.

FROM THE BOEING 314 TO THE JUMBO JET

On May 20, 1939, twelve years to the day after the historic solo flight by Charles Lindbergh, the Boeing 314 Yankee Clipper took off from the port of Port Washington, Long Island, New York, on the first commercial airline flight by a powered aircraft between the United States and Europe. Boeing had won the competition among American aircraft makers for an Atlantic flying boat, whereupon the two giants of American aviation officially sealed their long cooperation, which thirty-six years later led to the Jumbo Jet, by signing a contract for six Clipper flying boats on July 21, 1936. Mail and freight service was followed on June 28, 1939, by the first scheduled service by a passenger aircraft between the United States and Europe. The Dixie Clipper flew from New York via the Azores and Lisbon to Marseille in the south of France, while on July 8, 1939, the crew of the Yankee Clipper chose the northern route over Foynes, Ireland, to Southampton on the English Channel. During the Second World War, PAA and its Boeing 314s supported the American armed forces. In January 1943, one of PAA's Boeing 314s flew US president Franklin D. Roosevelt to a meeting with British prime minister Winston Churchill in the Moroccan Atlantic port of Casablanca.

The Boeing 307 Stratoliner, jointly commissioned by Transcontinental & Western Air (TWA) and PAA, was a second point of contact between Boeing and Pan American. The three aircraft ordered by PAA were called Clipper Rainbow, Clipper Comet, and Clipper Flying Cloud. The prop liner was based on the four-engine Boeing B-17 Flying Fortress and was the first commercial aircraft equipped with a pressurized cabin. It entered service on routes in the Caribbean and to South America, until, with the outbreak of the Second World War, it was also pressed into war service. PAA divested itself of its three aircraft in 1947, after more-modern and better-performing aircraft, such as the Douglas DC-4, became available. When in 1950 the airline officially changed its name from Pan American Airways Corporation (PAA) to Pan American World Airways, Inc. (Pan Am), it had already established a truly global network of routes with its Douglas DC-4s, its Lockheed L-049 Constellations, and, in particular, the legendary Boeing 377 Stratocruiser. This airliner was derived from the B-29 long-range bomber, and it offered onboard service that was unsurpassed in its day. A comfortable bar on the lower deck, reached by a spiral staircase, invited passengers to enjoy a drink, while on the main deck, beds that folded down from the ceiling and seats that turned into lounge beds provided a unique level of comfort. Pan Am's extravagant "The President" first-class service did the rest to make the Boeing 377 the symbol of luxury above the clouds. But all of this was just a small foretaste of the events of the mid-1950s, which were to lead to even closer cooperation between Boeing and Pan Am. Juan Trippe ultimately became the only airline chief to show interest in the four-jet 367-80 Dash 80 prototype as a future transport and airliner.

Boeing had established a major lead over all other American aircraft makers in the development of jet aircraft,

Half a century separates these two photos: the Martin M-130 flying boat China Clipper, with which PAA initiated scheduled air service across the Pacific on November 22, 1935, and the 747-121 N753PA Clipper Westwind, photographed in 1985. *Pan Am*

This drawing made for Pan Am shows the China Clipper landing in the harbor basin of the former British crown colony of Hong Kong—in the 1930s still without the backdrop of skyscrapers. *Pan Am*

The Boeing 314 flying boat was the first point of contact between PAA and Boeing. On May 20, 1939, the airline launched commercial airline service between the United States and Europe with the Boeing 314 Yankee Clipper. *Boeing*

with cruising speeds near the speed of sound. The required basic research data were captured by Allied troops in former secret German laboratories in Völkenrode, near Brunswick, after the end of the war. Under the leadership of leading American aerodynamicist Theodore von Kármán, whose team included Boeing's chief aerodynamicist George S. Schairer, American troops secured the booty that was found there. After returning to the United States, Schairer immediately halted development of the B-47 bomber, with its conventional unswept wing (in planning since 1943), and ordered it redesigned as a jet with sharply swept wings modeled on the basis of German research documents. The concept was further refined in the company's own high-speed wind tunnel, and on December 17, 1947, the Boeing Model 450-3-3 (XB-47), the first American jet bomber with swept wings, took to the air for the first time. This basic research not only gave the aircraft maker from Seattle an immense competitive advantage but also paved the way for the design of modern jet aircraft—including the 747.

PAA president Juan Trippe specified in the 1930s that his crew members should be equipped with uniforms in the maritime look. He established a tradition that lives on in air travel to the present day, even after Pan Am's bankruptcy in 1991. *Wolfgang Borgmann*

PAN AM FLIES INTO THE JET AGE

After lengthy negotiations, in which Boeing at first only reluctantly responded to Pan Am's demands, on October 13, 1955, Trippe ordered twenty examples of the Boeing 707, which had been developed from the Dash 80. On October 26, 1958, the Jet Clipper America, Pan Am's Boeing 701-121 with the registration N711PA, took off on the type's first commercial flight from New York to Paris. Pan Am initially ordered six examples of this basic version of the 707, which was later replaced on the North Atlantic routes by the more capable Boeing 707-320. In addition to the comfortable, fast flight above the clouds, for the first time, passengers on Pan Am's jet service were also able to enjoy another innovation: economy class.

Compared to tourist class, which had been introduced on piston-engine airliners in 1952, economy was at least 20 percent cheaper. The offer was well received: in the summer of 1964 there were 214 transatlantic flights on Pan Am's flight plan. One year later, it was already 258 flights—50 percent more than in the purely propeller age just a few years earlier. The well-utilized jets carried three times as many passengers as their predecessors with piston engines. There seemed to be no upper limit in the growth of air travel in the mid-1960s, and so for Juan Trippe there seemed to be just one answer: they had to have an even-larger jet

In the late 1940s, with its luxurious equipment and exclusive PAA "The President" service, the Boeing 377 Stratocruiser set new standards in transatlantic air travel. On its lower deck there was a cocktail lounge that could be accessed by a spiral staircase from the main deck during flight. *Boeing*

Pan American took off into the jet age with the Boeing 707-121. In the beginning, only company founder Juan T. Trippe showed any interest in the aircraft. Under pressure from Pan Am, Boeing designed a wider fuselage, which permitted the installation of six seats in a row instead of five. *Boeing*

Clipper Ocean Pearl on the ramp at New York's John F. Kennedy airport. In March 1986, this was the domain of the Boeing 747 and the supersonic Concorde. In the background can be seen a 747-121 with the registration N740PA painted in the billboard look. *Jon Proctor*

CHAPTER 2
ON THE WAY TO THE JUMBO JET

The story of the Boeing 747 began in August 1965, when Dick Rouzie received a telephone call for Boeing engineer Joe Sutter. The latter was vacationing at his summer retreat on the idyllic Hood Canal, not far from Seattle, when his neighbor suddenly appeared and gruffly announced: "Hey Sutter, they're calling for you on my telephone." The Sutter family's vacation home had no telephone, and so he had admonished his office to disturb him at his summer retreat with the help of his neighbor only in case of emergency. Dick Rouzie, then director of Engineering in the Boeing Transport Division, regarded his news as such a case—albeit in a positive way. On that day he offered Joe Sutter the project management for a new Boeing jet that was to surpass all previously known dimensions in civil aircraft design. This was the moment of the Jumbo Jet's birth. Joe Sutter began his career with Boeing in February 1946, and one of his first tasks was to make a success of the Boeing 377 Stratocruiser program, which was lagging behind. In addition to the pure engineering tasks, for the first time Sutter also had contact with airline customers, and in this case particularly with Pan American, which had initially ordered twenty brand-new Boeing 377s and was impatiently waiting for them to be delivered. These were the first contacts between Sutter and John Borger, who had joined Pan American in 1934, was named chief project engineer for all of the airline's aircraft procurement programs in 1946, became chief engineer and Juan Trippe's right-hand man in all technical matters in 1963, and from 1971 until his retirement in 1980 led the airline's technical department as vice president and chief engineer and member of the board.

Sutter also made a career with Boeing and after his Stratocruiser interlude led the aerodynamic team working on the Boeing 367-80, the Dash 80 test bed, and played a leading role in the design of the resulting KC-135 and Boeing 707 and the short- and medium-range Boeing 727 and 737 jet airliners. After his involvement with the smallest member of the Boeing family of jets, Sutter was now to work on the 747 as project manager. Not only was it the

In the competition of the beautiful noses, the 747-100 prototype N7470 is ahead of the Boeing 737-100 prototype, at least in perspective. Photo taken at the Museum of Flight at the Boeing company airfield at Renton. *Ted Hutter*

largest type, it was also by far the greatest challenge of his professional career. As with many previous Boeing designs, Pan American was the driving force behind the development of the future megaliner. After the orders by Pan Am founder and president Juan Trippe had already had a decisive influence on the success of the Boeing 314 flying boat, the luxurious 377 Stratocruiser, and the four-jet Boeing 707, Trippe again challenged Boeing management. If Boeing would guarantee to build the Jumbo Jet, with roughly two and a half times the passenger capacity of a 707, for his Pan American, he would promise an order for twenty-five of those megaliners. The request came at the right moment for Boeing, since the 707 that had been offered so far could not keep up with the growth in air traffic. Douglas had developed the competing DC-8 into the Super Sixty, which was capable of carrying about two hundred passengers across the Atlantic in a two-class configuration, but a comparable stretch of the 707 would have required lengthening of the undercarriage and thus considerable structural intervention in order to prevent the tail from striking the runway during takeoff and landing. Boeing management did not regard the required investment as economical and was therefore happy about Pan Am's interest in a completely new aircraft design.

When Sutter began with the detailed investigations, Boeing was engaged in two prestigious studies at the same time. The company was participating in the US Air Force tender for a transport aircraft called the C-5, with the then-unimaginable payload of more than 110 tons. Boeing was also engaged in development of the 2707 supersonic jet in competition with the Anglo-French Concorde. The 2707 was designed with complex variable-geometry wings to ensure sufficient lift in all speed ranges and was to be capable of transporting up to three hundred passengers at Mach 2.7. Internally, both projects enjoyed a higher priority than the timid beginnings of the 747 design. Sutter therefore had to be satisfied with twenty coworkers in the beginning—compared to five hundred colleagues working on the C-5 tender. Another special honor among Boeing engineers was being appointed to the 2707 team, since in the mid-1960s a great future was still predicted for supersonic air travel. Many insiders, on the other hand, regarded the gigantic 747 as a temporary interim solution rather than the ideal route for air transport. At the time when Pan American and Boeing presidents Trippe and Allen signed a letter of intent for twenty-five Boeing 747s on December 22, 1965, the internal weightings had shifted in favor of the 747 since the loss of the C-5 project, believed to be safe, to Lockheed. At that time, there was neither a fixed design nor an available power plant for the planned Jumbo Jet. The two projects, airframe and power plants, were begun in parallel. This was a first in civil aviation, since normally the development of power plants preceded that of the airframe by years. When Boeing decided on the Pratt & Whitney JT9D, this engine existed only on the paper of the Pratt & Whitney designers. "2.5" was regarded as the magic formula during 747 development. Compared to the earlier 707, the Jumbo was to be capable of carrying two and a half times as many passengers. For it, Pratt & Whitney

The father of the 747, Boeing engineering legend Joe Sutter, in front of an example of the Pratt & Whitney JT9D engine, which caused major problems at the start of the aircraft program. *Boeing*

The General Electric engine that powered the Lockheed C-5 Galaxy was also offered for the 747; however, it was less powerful than the Pratt & Whitney JT9D and would have enabled a cruise of just Mach 0.70 and not the Mach 0.85 demanded by Pan Am. *US Air Force photo, Tech. Sgt. Robert Cloys*

developed a power plant with 2.5 times the thrust of the most-powerful jet engines then available. Although the Boeing 747 was created on a blank sheet of paper and had no design parallels to the proposed C-5 design, the project profited from the preliminary work by the engine manufacturer for the US Air Force transport that later became known as the Lockheed C-5 Galaxy.

Structural assembly of the first 747-130 for Lufthansa, which was delivered to the airline in March 1970 with the registration D-ABYA and the name Nordrhein-Westfalen. *Boeing*

HANGING BY A THREAD . . . OR . . . HOW A DOUBLE-DECKER BECAME A WIDE BODY

When, following the letter of intent signed with Pan Am in December 1965, the Boeing management around CEO Bill Allen officially launched the 747 program, and just one month later Pan Am signed a binding sales contract for twenty-five aircraft at a price of six hundred million US dollars, the development team was under considerable time pressure. Pan Am requested that the first jets be delivered by the end of 1969, which in view of the great technological challenges seemed almost an impossibility. After all, there were just twenty-eight months between the start of the first project work and the required delivery date. Joe Sutter not only was under considerable time pressure but, to his disappointment, could fall back on only a small core team, since the Boeing Commercial Airplanes Division's personnel resources were extremely tight with the parallel development of the 2707 supersonic jet, the 737, the stretched 727-200, and the 747. Other parts of the company were also stretched to the limit through working on demanding military and space programs, such as construction of the NASA Saturn V lunar rocket. Sutter knew that airlines around the world were interested, not only in a new passenger jet but also in a large-capacity cargo transport. The container age with standardized 20- and 40-foot metal containers had first arrived in the shipping industry in 1956. Shippers as well as freight forwarders demanded that airfreight should also be included in the container transport chain to further expand rapid and cost-effective world trade. But no matter how one twisted and turned it, no sea container would fit into the large aircraft desired by Pan Am, with two narrow cabins one on top of the other. The alternative design of an extremely wide and high main deck with a cockpit located one floor higher and an upward-opening nose offered the only possibility. The resulting large cargo hold could thus be loaded and unloaded from the front in an efficient and time-saving manner. A 747 passenger version had become a quasi secondary product, with a passenger cabin with two aisles and up to ten seats in one row. After initially only handmade sketches of the revolutionary design were created due to lack of time, the cabin planners around Joe Sutter began to work out the basic design in detail. In this first concept phase the 747 quite incidentally received its characteristic appearance with the prominent upper deck, whose aft section is actually just an aerodynamically optimally

Taken in February 1989, this photo shows the static pressure tests carried out on 747 fuselages. In order to identify possible weak points in good time and to prevent dangerous cracks from forming, Boeing subjected a 747-200 bought back from Japan Air Lines and a brand-new 747-400 to thousands of simulated flights, in which the fuselages were alternately pressurized and depressurized again. *Boeing*

A view of the well-utilized 747 final assembly line during boom times. A complete aircraft factory exclusively for production of the Jumbo Jet was built in record time on the edge of Paine Field, a US Air Force base abandoned by the military in 1966, 35 miles north of Seattle. With a surface area of 4,284,036 square feet and a volume of 469 million cubic feet, the gigantic production hangar remains the largest building in the world. *Boeing*

The Lufthansa 747-230F freighter and its load look almost like a toy in this Boeing publicity photo, which was taken next to the gigantic final-assembly hangar at Everett. *Boeing*

shaped conclusion of the cockpit in front of it and was not planned from the outset as an area for an exclusive first-class lounge. Its unmistakable design, which Boeing patented in October 1968, also included wings with 37.5 degrees of sweep, which gave the Boeing 747 the high cruising speed of 499 knots desired by Pan Am. The Boeing 747 had initially been designed for a maximum takeoff weight of 375 tons, but from the start the Boeing engineers had given it the development potential for much-higher weights. This was also true of the undercarriage, whose eighteen wheels distribute the entire weight of the aircraft, up to the current 747-8 version (with its maximum takeoff weight of 975,105 pounds for the passenger version), so evenly on the surface that no damage can result to the parking areas, taxiways, or runways. Each of the four main undercarriage legs is equipped with four wheels, while the nosewheel leg has two wheels. Joe Sutter designed the 747 with the highest safety margin in civil aircraft construction at the time. This also included the undercarriage, which was controlled by four independent hydraulic systems. It also had electrical and manual backup systems in case the extension mechanism should fail. The main undercarriage is divided into two units installed under the fuselage and two under the wings, in order to distribute the forces evenly across the aircraft structure. If the jet lands unevenly or if the ground on the taxiways is uneven, a hydraulic system connecting all four landing-gear legs provides additional compensation for the loads that occur. In the event of an undercarriage failure, in an emergency a 747 can also land safely with just one functioning landing-gear leg on each side of the fuselage. In order to ensure safe braking of the jet, the 747-100 had an antilock braking system that automatically braked the wheels up to 1,600 times per second and then released again immediately. The braking procedure was assisted by the thrust reversers, manually operated by the pilot, which were present on all four power plants.

Despite all the Sutter team's euphoria to have come up with a market-driven 747 design that met the wishes of as many potential customers as possible, this idea initially met with great resistance from Boeing management. There the unanimous opinion prevailed that Juan Trippe expected, as he had requested, an aircraft with two passenger decks—and that Boeing should deliver precisely that. Otherwise, it was feared, Trippe would accuse Boeing of breach of contract and have his double-decker built by one of Boeing's competitors. Numerous examples from the past showed that this concern was not unfounded. Boeing, too, had experienced this uncompromising attitude on the part of Trippe in the 707 program. The aircraft's fuselage had to be redesigned and widened at a high investment cost, not least because of pressure from Pan Am, so that a maximum of six instead of the previous five passengers could be seated per row. But Sutter had no time for lengthy discussions with the customer about possible alternatives—and so he had to put all his eggs in one basket. A failure of the upcoming talks was out of the question—and would have threatened the entire aircraft program. Milt Heinemann, the Boeing cabin expert who was valued for his diplomatic

Taken at New York's JFK airport on August 30, 1971, this photo of Clipper Neptune's Favorite clearly illustrates the size difference between the dainty-looking engines of a Douglas DC-8-63 parked on the left of the photo and the Jumbo Jet's JT9D engines, with a diameter of 7.7 feet. *Jon Proctor*

negotiating skills, was chosen to be the bearer of the delicate news. He had previously developed the cabins of the 707 and 727 in cooperation with the design company Walter Dorwin Teague Associates. He was tasked with traveling to Pan Am company headquarters in New York and there convincing Trippe and Borger, in particular, of the idea of the wide-body jet. The day before his departure, the brilliant idea came to him, in addition to the usual drawings and technical data, to graphically illustrate the width of the cabin by using a suitable length of red clothesline, which he thought to unroll before the eyes of the Pan Am team. With the clothesline in his luggage, Heinemann set out on his delicate mission into the lion's den on the American East Coast. Since the Pan Am delegation had not arrived yet, he was able, as a test, to unroll the clothesline on the floor of the conference room chosen for the presentation. Heinemann could not believe his eyes—the planned diameter of the Jumbo Jet cabin exactly matched the width of the impressively large office in the Pan Am Building over Grand Central Terminal in Midtown Manhattan. With this knowledge up his sleeve, Heinemann tried to convince the initially very skeptical Juan Trippe and John Borger with dry facts about the new plans, but he was not entirely successful. The mood threatened to change when Heinemann played his wildcard. He handed one end of the clothesline to a stunned airline employee and told him to take it to the other end of the room. At first Trippe and Borger could not believe that this was in fact supposed to become the width of the new passenger jet, but their initial skepticism had given way to a certain curiosity. Boeing used this when, a short time later, the two leading Pan Am representatives paid a return visit to Seattle. In addition to a squat and dark, full-size mockup of the two-level design, as Pan Am originally wanted it, Bill Allen and Joe Sutter also showed them the full-size mockup of the main deck of their alternative wide-body jet. They subsequently inspected a replica of the upper deck. When Trippe asked what the area behind the cockpit was, Borger suggested that they could use it as a rest area for the crew on long-range flights. To the great relief of the members of the Boeing team present, Juan Trippe accepted the idea of the wide-body with the words "This will be reserved for our passengers." Development of the 747 as we know it today could begin.

Walter Dorwin Teague was one of the best-known American architects, illustrators, and graphic and industry designers. From 1926 until his death in 1960, he advised American companies in their product design and was thus the father of the modern corporate design. Teague designed cameras for Kodak, invented the elegant design of the legendary Steinway concert grand, defined the appearance of American long-distance trains, and in the 1930s shaped the image of Texaco gas stations across the United States. In view of a growing number of orders and employees, in 1945 Teague founded the Walter Dorwin Teague Associates (WDTA) design bureau. In addition to the company founder as owner, who was later joined by his son Walter Dorwin Teague Jr., leading associates could qualify for a WDTA partnership. Among these selected "associates" was the designer Frank Del Guidice, to whom Teague entrusted the establishment and management of the Seattle office, founded in 1946. WDTA had previously entered into a contract with Boeing for the design of the cabin of what was undoubtedly one of the most luxurious passenger aircraft of its day—the Boeing 377 Stratocruiser. Neither Teague nor Boeing could have suspected at that time that this unique symbiosis between an external design office and the current leading aerospace company would continue to the present day. Beginning with the 377, over the following seven decades Teague designed the passenger cabins of the Boeing 707, 720, 727, 737, 747, 757, 767, 777, and 787. This included the adaptation of the individual cabins to the continually evolving tastes of the time. Among the legendary Teague designs were, for example, the luxurious bar in the lower deck of the Stratocruiser, reached by a spiral stairway, the individual service modules with call buttons for the cabin crew, fresh-air nozzles, lamps and oxygen masks under the overhead luggage compartments of the 707, and the futuristic cabin design of the Boeing 787 Dreamliner.

But no airliner before or after enabled such a radical change in cabin architecture as the Boeing 747-100. With a height of 8 feet, a width of 20 feet, and a length of 185 feet, to the Teague team around Boeing office head Frank Del Guidice the cabin of the Jumbo Jet was a challenge and an opportunity at the same time. Together with Boeing, Teague developed service modules in the center of the fuselage, which consisted of either toilet blocks or catering stations. On the one hand, this had very practical reasons, since the walking distances for crew members were shortened and passengers waiting in front of the toilets did not hinder the service process, but also psychological aspects. After all, each economy-class passenger had only about a hundred other passengers in his visible surroundings, and thus no more than in a short-haul jet of the time. Thus, while the 747 was the first means of mass transport in aviation, it was not necessarily perceived as such by each individual passenger. While the Jumbo Jet was not the first aircraft type to offer in-flight movies and access to music by way of headphones, the sides of the service modules were ideally suited for the installation of big screens, which hindered neither crew nor passengers walking in the aisles. The cabin of the 747 thus became a flying movie theater or a comfortable lounge, since even in economy class, American Airlines, for example, offered comfortable seating for relaxing above the clouds. Not ordered by any airline, however, was the Tiger Lounge. Designed by Teague in the 1970s jungle look, its vertical window in the form of a glass bar was supposed to offer a view of the world beneath the belly of the Jumbo.

After firm orders from Pan Am for twenty-five aircraft and orders from Lufthansa, Japan Air Lines, and British Overseas Airways Corporation (BOAC), the construction of the final assembly line in the small city of Everett, about 31 miles north of Seattle, began in 1967. Like most aircraft projects, the 747 was also not spared development problems. After the aircraft design had been finalized, it had to "slim down" again in 1967 so that Boeing could meet the promised specifications. The entire structure was examined inch by inch for potential savings, and structural components were reduced or replaced by lighter materials. Last but not least, the 747's flight characteristics were decisive for its later success, and these were determined using large models in a total of 13,000 wind tunnel hours. As a result of the knowledge gained, Boeing changed the positioning of the engines (which were moved farther out on the wing), the engine pylons, and the landing flaps; planned new landing gear; modified the elevators and rudder; and changed the design of the tail to reduce drag. Parallel to the formation of its own production team, Boeing contracted 1,500 direct suppliers, which in turn received parts for 747 production from 15,000 subcontractors. As a percentage, 65 percent of the empty weight of the original 747 as well as 50 percent of the aircraft value came from outside companies. Another impressive number: the 747 program required the design and manufacture of 270,000 tools custom made for the Jumbo Jet.

A SUPER FACTORY FOR A SUPER JET

As gigantic as the aircraft itself was the infrastructure necessary to produce it. Since there was no room for a new 747 final assembly line on the existing company airfield at Renton, located on the southern outskirts of Seattle, Boeing acquired 778 acres of property in Everett, about 35 miles north of the West Coast metropolis, in order to build a completely new factory for the Jumbo Jet, with factory buildings and ramps for the newly completed aircraft. Boeing used the flight operations facilities of Paine Field, a former US Air Force base, on the edge of which the "cradle of the Jumbo Jet" was built in record time. The central building is the 747 final-assembly hangar, which to this day is the world's largest building by volume, 19,634,954 cubic feet, with a surface area of 43 acres. In the summer of 1966, Boeing vice president Malcolm Stamper was given the herculean task of building 747 production at Everett from nothing and meeting the delivery dates promised to Pan Am, beginning in late 1969. Until then there was only a gigantic wooded area on Puget Sound, which first had to

During its eventful life, the first 747 built by Boeing, with the registration N7470, for a time had the long row of windows in the upper deck, with which some 747-100s were retrofitted and which became standard on the further-developed 747-200. *Boeing*

Bill Allen speaking during the official handover ceremony of Lufthansa's first 747-130 at Boeing's Renton airfield. As the company's chief executive officer from 1945 to 1969, he had a special relationship with the German airline. Notable events that occurred during this time span included the first order by Lufthansa for the Rolls-Royce Conway turbofan engine for the 707-430, the first order for the 727 by a European customer, production of the 737 (which was significantly boosted by Lufthansa), the first order for the 747-100 passenger version from Europe, and the first order for the freight version of the Jumbo Jet. *Boeing*

be cleared and prepared for construction of the 747 factory. On behalf of Boeing, the excavators moved 121 million cubic feet of earth, which would have been enough to build a 9.8-foot wall between New York and Washington, DC. The first Boeing employees began working at Everett just six months after the start of construction. Within a year their number rose to 20,000, who were often on-site before their workplace was completed, to contribute to the success of the mammoth project. In recognition of this truly herculean task, internally Boeing described him and his team as "the Incredibles." Never before in American aviation history had such a large single project been financed by a company without government subsidies.

The core of 747 production originally consisted of three production areas, each 1,000 feet long and 300 feet wide. Two served Jumbo Jet final-assembly lines, while in a third the wing and fuselage sections were preassembled and equipped with systems. In the first years of production, from processing the first sheet metal to maiden flight, it took about twenty-one months to complete a Boeing 747, with final assembly's share being just two months. If one adds up all the parts, including the smallest bolts, a 747-100 consisted of about 4.5 million components, which were delivered by an extensive network of suppliers, who accounted for around 60 percent of the total aircraft, to Everett for final assembly. These included 1,500 main and 15,000 subsuppliers from forty-nine American states and six nations. The actual final assembly at Everett began with the joining of the wings and the wing box. Once this was completed, it moved to the next workstation, to be joined to the fuselage center section. However, it was not until the next station that the 747 took on its familiar appearance with the installation of the prominent nose, tail, and empennage sections. Finally, in this Final Body Join Position, 124 miles of power cables were installed and the leading-edge and landing flaps were fitted, as well as the undercarriage. From that moment on, the 747 moved on its own undercarriage, and after leaving the final-assembly building it underwent a cabin pressure test before proceeding to the paint hangar for application of the individual airline colors. After installation of the cabin equipment, the 747 was handed over to the delivery center, which, after ground and flight tests in the presence of airline representatives, receipt of FAA certification, and payment by the customer, handed the aircraft over to its new owners.

Final assembly at Everett began in September 1967 with the arrival of the first nose section produced at Boeing's Wichita factory. The next milestone was achieved in March 1968, when the first wing was removed from the wing jig. While the aircraft was moving inexorably toward its completion, at that time not a single Pratt & Whitney JT9D engine had yet run on the test bench! So, Boeing presented its new pride and joy to the world public at the official rollout on September 30, 1968, still without functioning power plants. The aircraft systems of the prototype, with the apt registration N7470, were activated for the first time in January 1969, and the operation of the undercarriage, control surfaces, and flaps was tested.

THE JT9D DISASTER

When Pan American World Airways president Juan Trippe and Boeing president Bill Allen signed a letter of intent for twenty-five Boeing 747s on December 22, 1965, there was no fixed design of the selected engine type, since it was a completely new development. When Boeing decided on the Pratt & Whitney JT9D as the first and initially exclusive engine type for the Jumbo Jet, the engine existed only on the paper of the Pratt & Whitney design department. The technical challenges faced by Pratt & Whitney were enormous, since with almost 2.5 times greater thrust than the most powerful civil jet engine extant, the American engine maker was advancing into new dimensions. The JT9D was chosen because General Electric, whose TF39-GE-1C turbofan engine—originally developed for the slower-flying C-5 Galaxy—produced a maximum of 43,015 pounds of thrust, could not offer a competitive product. At Pan Am's request, the Boeing 747 had been designed for the high cruise speed of Mach 0.85, which only the JT9D-3A installed in the 747-100, with its 46,940 pounds of thrust, made possible. Had Boeing selected the alternative GE engine, the aircraft would have been limited to a cruise of Mach 0.70. The size of the JT9D, like the Jumbo Jet itself, was decidedly imposing. At 7.7 feet, the diameter of the fan, made up of forty-six blades, was about twice that of the engines that powered the earlier 707. The ratio between the air mass flowing around the engine core and that flowing through it (bypass ratio) was 5:1. The encasing of the noises emanating from the engine core and the sound-absorbing cladding of the air intake resulted in a drastic reduction in engine noise produced by the 747 compared to first-generation long-range jets such as the Boeing 707 and Douglas

After the technical disaster with the first version of the Pratt & Whitney JT9D engine, Lufthansa chose the General Electric CF6 engine to power its Boeing 747-230 fleet, which began entering service in 1971. In this photo a CF6-50E engine is being overhauled at the Lufthansa technical base in Hamburg in 1979. *Vierkotten/Lufthansa*

DC-8. And the design of the new Jumbo Jet engine also offered another advantage: the usual smoke trails produced by the earlier jets during takeoff and landing largely became a thing of the past.

A JT9D engine was first tested in its future element in June 1968. The first prototype, the RA 001, took to the air for the first time on February 9, 1969, not on a 747 but mounted under a Boeing B-52 experimental aircraft. The FAA awarded the Boeing 747-100 its type certification on December 31, 1969, but that in no way meant that its JT9D engines were ready for day-to-day operation by their first-time customers. Test pilot Waddell, in particular, had major concerns that the change in angle of attack might cause the sensitive engines to fail immediately after takeoff. In order to have at least a small chance of survival in an emergency, he insisted on installation of large batteries in the test cabin, which in an emergency were to supply power to the electrical system and hydraulic pumps, which were normally supplied by the engines. Even if luckily everything went well on the first flight, first customer Pan Am felt the whims of the new JT9D engines on the planned commercial maiden flight from New York's JFK airport to London Heathrow on the evening of January 21, 1970. A defective engine had to be shut down before the aircraft reached the runway. Luckily, Pan Am had convinced Boeing to provide a replacement aircraft for this prestigious event. In the Pan Am hangar it was secretly given the defective 747's name Clipper Young America and reached London—albeit late—with no further complications. The episode could have gone down as an anecdote in the history books, but it was followed by an unprecedented series of breakdowns that discredited the aircraft itself and its JT9D engines. The basic problem was that the turbofan engines reacted to a reduction in power with a flow separation in the compressor stages, resulting in failure accompanied by a loud bang and a frightening flash of flame. As well, when the aircraft was at a high angle of attack, ovalization of the engine casings occurred, causing the fan blades to strike their sides, resulting in damage. Both problems were identified by Pratt & Whitney and countermeasures initiated, but even in airline service it remained an insurmountable problem for the early 747-100.

From January 1970 to April 1971, Pan Am alone reported 431 engine failures in daily operation by the twenty-five aircraft it had received. In five cases, several engines failed simultaneously, and twenty-five engines caught fire in flight. The reliability rate reached its absolute nadir in June 1970, with an average of 5.5 engine shutdowns per 1,000 flying hours. As launch customer, Pan Am was especially hard hit by these technical problems—but it was far from being the only airline. Other important early customers for the 747, such as BOAC, Lufthansa, TWA, and Japan Air Lines, found themselves facing the same challenges. The events of the early 1970s did considerable damage to the image of Boeing and its 747, and that of the Jumbo Jet customers, since it was not uncommon for the safety of crews and passengers to be threatened. The fact that there were no serious incidents or even accidents as a result of these technical deficiencies was due not least to the excellently trained technical staffs and crews of the airlines concerned.

Lufthansa's chief technical officer, Reinhardt Abraham, described this situation from the customer's point of view on the occasion of the delivery of the one hundredth Boeing jet to Lufthansa on February 16, 1973, as follows: "Ninety-nine Boeing aircraft have flown for us and our subsidiary Condor on our route network, which is now the fourth largest in the world, and of these ninety-nine aircraft at least ninety-six have never disappointed us. As for the remaining three, and of course these are the first Jumbos of the 1970 vintage, on this day we are almost inclined to forgive and forget. But I don't want to deny that the commissioning of the B747 caused us major technical and economic problems."

With that, the JT9D is in good company, since it is a recurrent phenomenon in the aerospace industry that numerous civil engine types, even after they have been approved by the authorities, do not meet the expectations placed on them, and often endanger the lives of crews and passengers. If one looks back to the 1940s, the Lockheed

In contrast to Boeing, Lockheed selected the Rolls-Royce RB211 engine as the exclusive power plant for its L-1011 wide-body jet. Technical problems and the temporary bankruptcy of the engine maker brought the entire TriStar program into discredit and cost the company numerous potential customers—such as Lufthansa, which instead chose the DC-10 from McDonnell Douglas. *Pan Am*

L-049 Constellation had to be temporarily grounded after its Curtiss-Wright R-3355 piston engines developed fire hazard properties in the truest sense of the word. Boeing's chief test pilot, Edmund "Eddie" Allen, and his crew fell victim to it on February 18, 1943, when, after extinguishing a first engine fire, a second engine caught fire and the Boeing B-29 prototype failed to make the runway at Renton, Boeing's company airfield, and crashed into a meat-packing plant just short of the runway. On the other hand, the failure of the British Bristol 175 Britannia long-range transport was caused by the seemingly insurmountable technical problems of the Bristol Proteus 765 turboprop engine, offered exclusively for this type. Not until 1957, five years after the prototype's first flight, was BOAC able to place the type, which had begun so hopefully as an economical transatlantic airliner, into service. By then, however, the jet age was at the door, and even BOAC had lost interest in the slower propeller-driven aircraft. Technical problems and delays in the RB211 high-bypass turbofan engine program associated with the engine maker's temporary insolvency were the main reasons why this technically advanced type was outsold by the competing McDonnell Douglas DC-10 in the early 1970s. The RB211 had initially been chosen as the type's sole power plant. And if one looks to the present, almost all of the modern, fuel-efficient turbofan engines that power the Airbus A320neo, A-350, and A380 and the Boeing 787 and 777X series have been plagued by technical failures and project delays. Thus in 2018 it was not seventeen Jumbo Jets as in 1969, but hundreds of completed A320neo airliners that were in storage, because Pratt & Whitney and the CFM International Consortium of Safran and General Electric were unable to deliver sufficient numbers of usable engines. In the summer of 2019, the misery across all manufacturers and types had assumed such dimensions that Tim Clark, head of the influential Gulf carrier Emirates Airlines, threatened not to issue orders for new jets until he could be sure that the ordered aircraft were capable of delivering what the airframe and engine makers promised: to transport paying passengers reliably and safely.

"Give us aircraft and engines that function from day one. If you can't do that, then don't build them." —Tim Clark, CEO of Emirates Airlines in the summer of 2019.

HANGING BY A THREAD

After the initial euphoria following the Pan Am order, the airline industry quickly realized that the 747 was too daring a leap in size compared to the smaller DC-8 and 707 long-range jets. An increase in maximum takeoff weight from 150 to 340 metric tons (165 to 375 tons) and the associated two and a half times greater passenger capacity were simply too great for the airlines to be able to fill with passengers and freight the Jumbos they had ordered, and thus to achieve economical operation. This realization was especially bitter for Boeing, whose order book quickly found itself in free fall after the first promising orders. With a production capacity of twelve aircraft per month, the manufacturer was able to book 144 orders for its future flagship by the end of 1967, but the numbers collapsed dramatically in the following years. Just nineteen aircraft were sold in 1968—one year later it was twenty-two, followed by twenty in 1970. In 1971 Boeing succeeded in selling just seven aircraft, and a meager eighteen orders for the 747 were received in 1972. If the slump in orders continued, Boeing threatened to run out of money. To make matters worse, in 1969 seventeen completed Boeing 747s sat on the ramp at Everett, with concrete blocks hanging from their engine pylons instead of the JT9D engines, which had not been delivered. With great effort, Boeing was able to obtain enough sufficiently reliable engines from Pratt & Whitney to at least power the five 747-100s carrying out the flight test program—but delivery of the first jets to Pan Am and payment of the purchase price were out of the question. To make matters worse, a test aircraft was badly damaged while landing on the very short runway of Boeing's Renton airfield, when test pilot Ralph Cokely touched down a few meters short. The starboard wing undercarriage was badly damaged, but the pilot was able to keep the aircraft on the runway.

While the Lufthansa 747-130 had just three cabin windows on each side of the upper deck, the following 747-230B had ten, which was a good way to distinguish the two Jumbo versions, which at first glance looked quite similar. *LH-Bildarchiv/Lufthansa*

In 1966, Boeing was still regarded as the leading aviation and space concern in the world, and prestigious projects such as the Saturn V moon rocket, the 2707 supersonic airliner, and the 747 created a spirit of optimism; however, the events of 1969 caused the company to fear the worst. Boeing president Thornton Wilson, who in 1969 had taken over the post of chief executive officer from Bill Allen, relied on the daily benevolence of the creditor banks, after the accumulated debt exceeded the company value, in large part due to the 747 program, which had gone into a spin. Before the banks and the external consultants took over the reins of the company, Wilson made cuts of more than one hundred million US dollars in the form of an austerity program. This saved Boeing, but it would be years before the company and the economy of Seattle would recover from the resulting personnel and economic clear-cutting.

THE JUMBO JET TAKES OFF

On February 9, after extensive taxiing trials and satisfied with the technical state of the City of Everett aircraft, the crew selected for the maiden flight—consisting of Boeing test pilot Jack Waddell, copilot Brien Wygle, and flight engineer Jess Wallick—felt confident that the day of the first flight had come. Asked about his first impressions immediately after landing, still standing at the foot of the aircraft stairs a relieved Waddell answered with these traditional words: "The aircraft flies like a pilot's dream."

The 747 is one of the most intensively tested commercial aircraft types of all time. Ground and component tests in other aircraft types were followed by 1,400 hours of flying in the actual certification program before the 747 received its certification from the FAA in December 1969. More than a hundred additional test flights were required before the 747-200B version received its type certification. Boeing began the first component tests in 1967, such as the installation of 747 cockpit windows in a Boeing 707 experimental aircraft. The flap system, which made possible the aircraft's low approach speeds, and the inertial navigation system, which for the first time enabled autonomous position determination and thus made the navigator superfluous, were also tested on board a 707 test bed. By the time of the Jumbo Jet's maiden flight, therefore, Boeing could be relatively certain that the components and systems, which had been put through their paces in advance, would prove themselves in the 747-100. Boeing carried out the flight test program with five aircraft, one of which was provided with a fully equipped cabin for route-proving flights. The fuselages of the other four aircraft were filled with test instrumentation weighing several tons and 176 interconnected water tanks, with whose help the different positions of the center of gravity in the cabin could be measured. Before certification was issued, the test aircraft were also exposed to extreme flight conditions, such as speeds of up to 650 mph, altitudes of 44,950 feet, and critical maneuvers that were outside the parameters of regular scheduled flight operations.

After Boeing had obtained the first tangible performance data from the flight tests, and the test pilots had gained extensive flight experience, the next step was to pass this knowledge on to the flight crews of the customer airlines. To do this, the manufacturer established the Boeing College of Jet Knowledge—Superjet Branch. In contrast to a regular flight school, not only highly experienced pilots and flight engineers from the customer airlines were familiarized with the new type, but also ground personnel who in the future would service and maintain the aircraft. The first graduates of the Superjet Branch were Boeing's own instructors, who then passed their expert knowledge on to the airline crews. While the pilots were at school in the Boeing Flight Center in Everett, the ground personnel were receiving their 747 qualification in Renton. For the first time, the maker produced training for a new Boeing type in such a way that only standard and emergency procedures, in Boeing jargon "standard behavioral objectives," which the crews would have to reckon with in future everyday flight operations, were communicated intensively. From Boeing's point of view, however, detailed background information on specific systems and components was of secondary importance and, at best, supplementary information. Theoretical instruction was followed by about fifteen hours of flight training in the simulator, followed by the first flights in a "real" aircraft. "Surprisingly the crews are familiar with the greater distance between the cockpit and the ground after just two flights," according to a contemporaneous Boeing circular. Boeing also scheduled just two or three flights until the final-check flight in the presence of an FAA check pilot resulted in the 747 entry in the licenses of the airline crews. Thus qualified, they returned to their airlines around the globe and there trained other crew members to fly the Jumbo Jet.

A Swissair Boeing 747-357(M) above the peaks of the Swiss alpine mountains. *ETH-Bibliothek Zuerich*

CHAPTER 3 A SELECTION OF THE FIRST CUSTOMERS

PAN AMERICAN WORLD AIRWAYS (PAN AM)

Launch customer Pan Am planned its first commercial 747 flight to take place on the evening of January 21, 1970, from New York's John F. Kennedy Airport to London Heathrow. One week earlier, the wife of the American president, First Lady Pat Nixon, had christened the aircraft selected for this event Clipper Young America at the airport of the American capital. Instead of the usual champagne, colored water in the national colors red, white, and blue was sprayed on the nose of the aircraft. At the urging of Pan Am, Boeing did everything possible to ensure that, in addition to Clipper Young America, a second aircraft was also available—just in case. It was a decision that was to prove to be absolutely right for the reputations of Boeing and Pan Am, since an overheating and damaged engine forced the first aircraft to return to the gate before it reached the runway. After the passengers disembarked, the aircraft was towed into a Pan Am maintenance hangar, and there, in the hope that no one would notice the trick, it was swapped for the replacement aircraft N736PA Clipper Victor, hidden in the hangar. To help the charade succeed, behind the closed hangar doors Pan Am technicians even stuck the name of the unserviceable Clipper Young America on the replacement Jumbo. Pan Am invited the guests of honor, including Atlantic pioneer Charles A. Lindbergh, to dine in an elegant restaurant near the airport, while the replacement aircraft for the second attempt at the Pan Am premiere was towed to the gate and there loaded with the onboard meals for the Atlantic crossing. Passing angry, chanting demonstrators in front of the Pan Am hangar, who warned against a flight in the Boeing Jumbo and called it a modern version of the *Titanic*, the guests of honor, who were in high spirits, returned to board the replacement 747 for the second attempt. Six hours behind schedule, the new Clipper Young America took off on the now-uneventful flight to the Old World.

The look developed specifically for the jet age by the two American architects Edward Larabee Barnes and Charles Foberg gave the 747-121s flown by Pan American World Airways an extremely elegant appearance. *Norbert Andrup*

Clipper Young America's subsequent service with Pan American World Airways was less happy. After becoming the first Jumbo Jet to be commandeered by armed hijackers on August 5, 1970, and forced to fly to Cuba, this 747-121 was subsequently renamed Clipper Victor and on March 27, 1977, was destroyed in the collision of two Jumbo Jets at the Los Rodeos airport on the Canary Island of Tenerife. With 583 dead, it remains to this day the greatest loss of life in commercial aviation sans terrorist involvement.

Pan Am operated thirty-four passenger versions of the original 747-100. Thirty were new-production aircraft, two were 747-123s obtained from American Airlines, and two were 747-132s originally leased by Pan Am to Delta Air Lines. In addition to these pure passenger jets, five freighters also flew in Pan Am colors—three 747-121Fs built for the airline and two former American Airlines 747-123Fs. There were also seven 747-212B passenger aircraft previously flown by Singapore Airlines, two 747-221F freighters, and one 747-200C Combi, which was ultimately used by Pan Am exclusively for airfreight. Pan Am ordered eleven examples of the 747SP ultra-long-range version, and deliveries began in 1976.

THE 747SP OR "SUTTER'S BALLOON"

Like the 747-100, the Special Performance or SP version also went back to a requirement by Pan American World Airways. Pan Am's route between New York and Tokyo was a great success at the beginning of the 1970s, but the 747-121s used on the route lacked the range to serve the route without a refueling stop en route. And so, Pan Am turned not only to Boeing but also to McDonnell Douglas and Lockheed, hoping to receive an offer for an ultra-long-range version of their DC-10 and L-1011 wide-body jets. The 747's two competitors had even less range than the 747-100, and theoretical developments of the two types were still in the distant future. The 747 therefore remained the only type in the race, and Joe Sutter made it suitable for ultra-long-range routes, by giving it not only more-powerful engines—which were not yet available—but also a shorter fuselage and thus lower structural weight.

These studies led to the 747 Short Body—SB, which because of its curiously stout appearance quickly led to the nickname "Sutter's balloon" among Boeing workers. The decision to proceed with the short 747 was made while Joe

In the Pan American Experience's 100 percent accurate replica, one can re-create the exquisite experience of a flight in Pan Am 747 first class. This photo shows the cabin service in the upper deck of the Jumbo, with dishes made using the original Pan Am catering department recipes from the 1970s. *Pan Am Experience*

Boeing 747-212B *China Clipper II*, a name that recalled Pan Am's pioneering days. The original PAA *China Clipper* initiated regular air service across the Pacific on November 22, 1935. *Jon Proctor*

Sutter and Pan Am technical director John Borger were having dinner. Between the appetizers and the main course, the two exchanged handmade sketches of the new jet and its performance data, and when the two technical experts, who had become friends over many years of working together, parted, "all" that remained was to convince their bosses of their ideas. This happened the following day. It was exciting for Joe Sutter, after he was excluded from the decisive meeting of the Boeing board of directors and only afterward learned that the discussion, which went on for hours, revolved solely around the subject that the latest version of the 747 could not be called "Sutter's balloon," and that its name was to be changed to Special Performance—SP. As curious as the SP looked, it lived up precisely to expectations. The aerodynamic forces acting on the new design meant that Boeing could not limit itself to shortening the original 747-100. Redesign work was required, especially on the tail, in order to counteract the decrease in the yaw moment arm of the shorter fuselage. Since the new short Jumbo was also lighter than the basic version, it was possible

to simplify the design of the landing flaps, and the 747SP has a simple flap system instead of the original triple-slotted flaps. Joe Sutter placed great emphasis on ensuring that the flight characteristics of the 747SP were identical to those of the original Jumbo variants—and so from the pilot's point of view, the Special Performance is just another 747.

Its first flight on the route for which it was designed, between New York and Tokyo, took place on April 26, 1976. With a flight time of thirteen hours and forty minutes, this nonstop link, possible only because of the new 747SP, was almost four hours shorter than the previously offered service with a refueling stop. This Pan Am service quickly became so popular that the flight, which travelers quickly named the "New Orient Express," had to be increased from three times per week to a daily frequency. Pan Am placed the 747SP in service on its routes from San Francisco to Australia and New Zealand. On May 1, 1976, the Pan Am 747SP Clipper Liberty Bell made a record-breaking flight around the globe. Carrying ninety-six passengers, the Clipper took forty-six hours to circle the globe, with two fuel stops: at the Indian capital of New Delhi and Tokyo. In doing so, it beat the old record by 15.5 hours! Although the 747SP, like no other type from the Jumbo family, was customized not just for a single customer but for a specific route, Boeing was able to sell forty-five examples to Pan Am and other airlines around the globe that, like Pan Am, had a requirement for a wide-body jet for extremely long ranges. And so brand-new 747SPs flew in the colors of Braniff, CAAC,

The Hamburg airport was also once a destination for the Pan Am Jumbos. When the *Clipper Sovereign of the Seas* landed at Fuhlsbüttel for the first time on April 29, 1985, Pan Am planned to make Hamburg its hub for US traffic in northern Europe. This was to remain wishful thinking, however. *Hamburg Airport*

When Pan Am gave its 747SP-21 the traditional name China Clipper, it was planning to use the ultra-long-range version of the Jumbo on routes to the Chinese capital of Peking and to Shanghai. Pan Am

One can experience what it was like to travel in business class on a Pan Am 747-121 on board the Pan Am Experience at the gates of Los Angeles at flight level zero. *Pan Am Experience*

China Airlines, Iran Air, Iraqi Airways, Korean Air, Quantas, Saudia, South African Airways, Syrianair, TWA, and the emirs of Abu Dhabi.

TRANS WORLD AIRLINES (TWA)

The airline founded as Transcontinental & Western Air in 1930 and renamed Trans World Airlines in 1948 was the second customer for the Boeing 747. Beginning in 1970, it received a total of sixteen Boeing 747-131s and three 747SP-31s straight from the factory, and over the years these were supplemented by 747-100s and -200s purchased secondhand, causing its fleet of Jumbos to temporarily rise to thirty-seven aircraft. The B747-136 with the registration N93119 gained sad notoriety on July 17, 1996, when, as TWA 800, it took off from New York's John F. Kennedy airport for Paris Charles de Gaulle and after a few minutes in the air crashed in a fireball into the Atlantic off the coast of Long Island. The cause of the accident has since been hotly disputed by conspiracy theorists, who refuse to accept the official report by the investigating committee, which consisted of representatives of the National Transportation Safety Board (NTSB), the FBI, and the CIA. After the salvaged wreckage of the Jumbo Jet's fuselage was painstakingly reassembled like a giant puzzle, it was possible to determine that defective cable insulation probably led to a spark that caused the highly flammable oxygen-air mixture in the almost empty center fuel tank to explode. The exact spot where the mixture ignited was never found, but this assumption seemed the most plausible. In contrast, eyewitness accounts reporting the ascent of a surface-to-air missile and the shooting down of the aircraft were not taken into consideration. This thesis is also supported by the fact that investigators found traces of a plastic explosive between the rows of seats in the recovered wreckage, which could have been left by a bomb on board or by the aircraft being shot down. It will probably never be fully explained whether the theories of the conspiracy theorists or the assumptions of the official investigation committee correspond to the truth. As a direct result of the crash of TWA 800 and other fuel tank explosions, which took place on board Boeing 737 jets in 1990 and 2001 as well as on a Boeing 727 in 2006, in 2008 the FAA in the United States and the European EASA directed operators and manufacturers of commercial aircraft to take countermeasures. The required modifications affected machines under development as well as newly built machines and also included aircraft already in use that were approved after January 1, 1992.

Ever since it was founded, and especially after Howard Hughes acquired a majority of shares in 1939, TWA was frequently a force behind the development of new aircraft types. Such famous types as the Douglas DC-2, Boeing 307 Stratoliner, Lockheed L-049 Constellation, and Convair CV 880 were tailor-made at the suggestion and for the special requirements of the airline. TWA outlived its fiercest competitor Pan Am by ten years and in 2001 was acquired by American Airlines.

The livery introduced by TWA in 1977, with the red double stripes down the sides, was already the second look of this Boeing 747-131. *Jon Proctor*

TWA was the second customer for the Boeing 747 and received the aircraft seen here (with the registration N93114) new from the manufacturer in November 1970. It remained with the TWA fleet for just a short time, however, and in 1975 was sold to Boeing, where it was converted into a freighter with a refueling system in the nose and was disposed of to the Iranian air force. It apparently still exists there to this day, though probably grounded, with the serial 5-8105. *Jon Proctor*

Commemorative wine glass from TWA's 1970 inaugural 747 flight from New York to Paris. *Constance Marie Piccone collection*

LUFTHANSA: FIRST CUSTOMER FOR THE JUMBO FREIGHTER

Lufthansa's ordering of the Jumbo freighter in March 1969 proved to be a visionary decision. With a payload of up to 99 tons, the 747-230F was capable of carrying about three times the cargo tonnage of the previously used Boeing 707-330C. In addition to the distinctive hinged nose, the 747-230F with the registration D-ABYE, delivered on March 10, 1972, was the first cargo aircraft with an automatic loading system in the cargo hold. The principle remains the same today: electric-powered rollers recessed in the floor bring the pallets and containers into position in the Jumbo freighters via guide rails and switches. Even the 40-foot standard shipping containers fit on board a Jumbo freighter. Two days after it was christened Cargonaut, on April 19, 1972, it replaced the 707 on the Frankfurt–New York route. This first 747-230F laid the foundation for the leading role that Lufthansa Cargo AG now holds in the world airfreight market. Not until December 2004 did it finally retire its fleet of 747-230Fs, replacing the Jumbos with the Boeing MD-11, which was more fuel efficient.

Above left: The Jumbo freighter with the folding nose that gives it its "grin." The folding nose makes it possible to load and unload the aircraft from the front and was the main reason why the 747 development team around Joe Sutter placed the cockpit one floor above the main deck. *LH-Bildarchiv/ Lufthansa*

Below left: Starting in April 1972, Lufthansa's sole 747-230F until 1978 flew the route between Frankfurt/Main and New York six times per week, with a maximum payload of 88 tons. By comparison, the Boeing 707-330F, which it replaced, was capable of carrying only 33 tons. Even greater was the difference in cargo hold volume of 6,780 cubic feet (707), compared to the 34,608 cubic feet of the 747. *Werner Krüger / Lufthansa*

Right: The 747-230F(SCD) with the registration D-ABYO was the first Lufthansa Jumbo freighter with an additional side-loading door. Named Amerika, the aircraft joined the fleet in November 1978. After it was retired by Lufthansa in 2004, and several changes of owner, it ended up with Rayyan Air of Pakistan, which had it scrapped at Karachi in May 2014. *Werner Krüger / Lufthansa*

YO
D-ABYO
Lufthansa Cargo

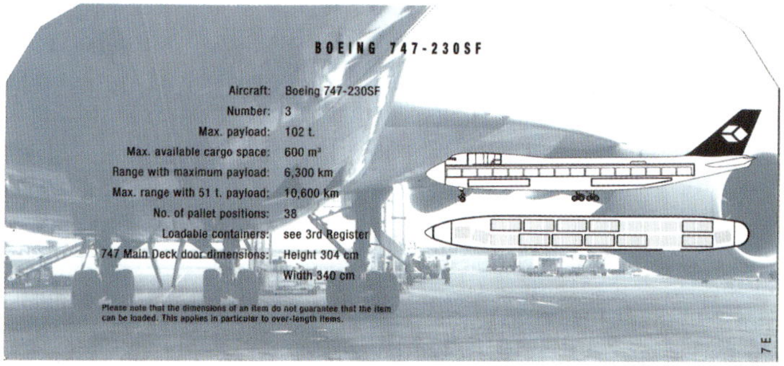

Above left: The 747-230M with the construction number 22363 was delivered to Lufthansa in the combi configuration with the registration D-ABYT and the name Hamburg in November 1980. After its retirement ten years later, it was converted into a dedicated freighter and from then on flew for German Cargo as a 747-230SF. Founded by Lufthansa in 1977 to expand the charter market, the freight airline was based in Kelsterbach at the Frankfurt airport and operated a mixed fleet of Boeing 707, 737, and 747 aircraft and Douglas DC-8-73s on its network of routes. In 1998, Lufthansa Cargo AG emerged from German Cargo Service GmbH, and it did not retire its last Boeing 747F until 2004. *Lufthansa*

Below left: On closer examination, what at first glance looks like a large hole in the area of the forward passenger stairs turns out to be an opened passenger door with a dark cover. The three Lufthansa passenger-freight combis converted into pure freighters operated by German Cargo, with the registrations D-ABYT, D-ABYW, and D-ABYY, had just the side cargo door for loading of the main deck. *Lufthansa*

Above right: Released by German Cargo, this sketch illustrates the loading of the 747-230SF's main with freight containers. *Wolfgang Borgmann collection*

Opposite: In this photo the 747-130F that would later be registered D-ABYE has the temporary American registration it wore during certification flights by Boeing. *Boeing*

Lufthansa Cargo

After the founding of Lufthansa Cargo AG in 1993, the 747-230SFs of the former German Cargo (*in background*) and Lufthansa's 747-230Fs flew in the standard livery of the new freight airline with the crane emblem. *Lufthansa Cargo*

The special livery worn by Lufthansa Cargo AG's 747-230Fs from 1998 to 2003 was called Service Revolution. Named Afrika, the aircraft joined Lufthansa on October 24, 1986, and was sold to Air Atlanta Icelandic in 2004. *Werner Krüger / Lufthansa*

A BLOCK CHANGE FOR THE 747-400

Scarcely had the small 737 City Jet fledged, with Lufthansa's help, when Boeing brought its gigantic counterpart to the market. After the initial order by Pan Am, Lufthansa was the first customer outside the United States, with a small order for three Jumbo Jets. The airline's passengers, used to smaller jets with a single central aisle, were beside themselves with enthusiasm. The first-class lounge in the upper deck, accessible via a spiral staircase, the high and wide main cabin with two aisles, just nine seats per row in tourist class, the sonorous drone of the JT9D turbofan engines—the hitherto unknown flight experience elicited spontaneous applause even from frequent fliers when the super bird took off. Lufthansa began scheduled service with its first 747-130s on April 26, 1970. And there was another first associated with it. For the first time, passengers on board a Lufthansa jet could select various music channels via headset and amuse themselves with motion pictures during flight. The 747-130 was capable of accommodating 361 passengers.

Thanks to the Jumbo Jet, flying with Lufthansa lost its exclusivity and paved the way to the modern "global village." The first 747-130s, whose troublesome engines caused Lufthansa serious problems, were followed in 1971 by the improved 747-230B, an improved pure passenger version with greater range and payload.

This did not end the 747 era for Lufthansa, however, since its technical department played a significant role in the development of two advanced versions, the 747-400 and the 747-8. The 400 of the 1980s goes back to the initiative of leading managers of the Lufthansa technical department, including the later Lufthansa chairman of the board of the Management and Supervisory Board Dr. Jürgen Weber. Together with technical luminaries of the company, such as Dr. Rolf Stüssel and Dr. Klaus Nittinger, Jürgen Weber considered how Lufthansa could bring its longtime partner Boeing to abandon the piecemeal tactic, which was regarded with concern, when it came to the 747. While Boeing showed interest only in further developing its jumbo gradually, which the manufacturer could accomplish in small steps without great engineering expenditure, Lufthansa was demanding a new version of the Jumbo with all of the new technologies then available for use in civil aircraft. To push through this version, called the Block Change, in 1985 Lufthansa joined with the technical departments of British Airways, Cathay Pacific, KLM, Northeast, Quantas, and Singapore Airlines, which had likewise been disappointed by Boeing's plan to develop the 747 in small steps. A cautionary example to them was the 747-300, whose principal difference from the -200 was merely a lengthened upper deck. It had less range than its predecessor, and sales were therefore sluggish.

The airline alliance's demands for a reworked, modern Boeing 747 included winglets on the wingtips for improved aerodynamics and reduced fuel consumption; modern materials for weight savings; a flexible cabin arrangement; new digitally controlled power plants such as the general Electric CF6-80, Pratt & Whitney 4000, or Rolls-Royce RB211; and a modern two-man glass cockpit, which, for the first time in a Jumbo Jet, was to incorporate computer displays. Boeing yielded to the arguments of potential customers, and it was rewarded with orders for the 747-400, which, with 694 sold, made it the most successful model of the Jumbo. The most striking feature of the 747-400 is its 5.9-foot upturned winglets, but what mattered most to the airlines were the details hidden from the eyes of the passengers, such as the reduction in the number of switches and instruments in the cockpit from about a thousand to fewer than four hundred. This digitization eliminated the need for a flight engineer, required in all previous models, whose tasks had now been largely taken over by the onboard electronics. Work on the first aircraft began at Everett in September 1987, and rollout of the first prototype took place on January 26, 1988. The 747-400 flew for the first time four months later, on April 29. Four aircraft took part in the flight test program, which resulted in three type certifications. The version with Pratt & Whitney power plants received its certification on January 9, 1989; the version powered by four General Electric engines followed on May 18; and the Rolls-Royce variant was certified on

June 8. On January 26, 1989, the first 747-400, registration N661US, was delivered to Northwest. After the merger between Northwest and Delta Air Lines, the aircraft continued flying in the latter's colors and is now displayed in the Delta Flight Museum at the Atlanta airport. In addition to the pure passenger version, the 747-400 could be ordered as a freighter, a combined freight-passenger version, a short-range version for the Japanese domestic market, and a version for extreme long ranges. After the first aircraft were retired from passenger service, in 2004 Boeing launched, in cooperation with outside partners, a freighter conversion program under the name 747-400 Boeing Converted Freighter. The aircraft retained the lengthened upper deck and were equipped with just a side freight door and a freight-loading system. Israel Aerospace Industries also converted former 747 passenger jets into 747-400BDSF (BeDek Special Freighter) freighters, which also had no nose cargo door.

747-8: THE ULTIMATE JUMBO JET

When Lufthansa began scheduled services between Frankfurt and Washington, DC, with the Boeing 747-8 Intercontinental on June 1, 2012, it was more than a typical maiden flight. Scarcely any other type in the Lufthansa fleet had been continually developed and improved over the decades in such close cooperation between the aircraft maker and the airline as the legendary Jumbo Jet. Lufthansa was also godmother to the Dash 8 and, as the first customer for the 747-8 Intercontinental passenger version, has made a decisive contribution to countless details of what was then, at 250 feet, the longest commercial aircraft in the world. Externally, the 747-8 was still unmistakably a Jumbo, with its unique silhouette. But a look inside the 747-8 revealed that there was, in part, a newly developed aircraft behind the familiar design. The new queen of the skies came quietly. Adopted from the Boeing 787, its four General Electric GEnx-2B engines, the exclusive power plants of the 747-8, produced a noise footprint that had been reduced by about a third compared to the previous 747-400 version. It

Photographed at Everett in spring 1970, the first Jumbo for Lufthansa during final preparations for its delivery flight. *Boeing*

Lufthansa

Left: The last two letters of the future German registration D-ABYA are already present on the nosewheel doors as the 747-130 lifts off on one of the final test flights at the Boeing company airfield at Renton, wearing a temporary US registration. *Boeing*

Above: The Boeing worker sitting next to the model gives some idea of the impressive size of this model of a 747-230M. Lufthansa used it for publicity work and to plan the future use of the combis it had ordered. *Boeing*

Above right: Meeting of two heavyweights for the so-called C check in the Lufthansa technical hangar at Frankfurt airport. Larger maintenance events on the Lufthansa 747 fleet are the responsibility of its partners in the ATLAS alliance. *Jürg Andermatt / Lufthansa*

Right: Within the ATLAS maintenance alliance formed between it and Air France, Alitalia, and Sabena in 1969, Lufthansa was responsible for overhauling the JT9D engines and later also for the CF6-50. The general overhaul of the Boeing 747 was carried out by Air France and, after its entry in 1972, also by the Spanish airline Iberia. *Gerd Rebenich / Lufthansa*

Lufthansa
YJ

Left: Last finishing touches on the 747-230M D-ABYJ prior to delivery of the wide-body jet to Lufthansa. Lufthansa used this same registration on one of its 747-8s of the latest generation of Jumbo Jets. *Boeing*

Above: Lufthansa joined forces with other potential first customers of the 747-400 to convince Boeing to produce a Block Change version of the Jumbo Jet incorporating all the then-available advances in aviation technology. *Ingrid Friedl / Lufthansa*

Right: Three times Lufthansa aviation history in one picture. The 747-230B in the photo is just as much history as is the Lufthansa livery used between 1968 and 1988. Hong Kong's Kai Tak airport, where the Jumbo is about to land, also belongs to history. *Dietmar Plath / Lufthansa*

The classic 747 of the first Jumbo generation not only spurred mass tourism but, thanks to its large freight capacity, also took part in the steady expansion of intercontinental trade in the 1970s and 1980s. *Astrovision*

Northwest Airlines was the first customer for the 747-400. The aircraft illustrated here with the registration N663US was delivered to Northwest on January 26, 1989, the 715th Jumbo Jet to be built. After its merger with Delta Air Lines, the wide-body jet continued in service in Delta colors. *Norbert Andrup*

Lufthansa also used the registration from its first 747-130 for the current 747-8 flagship of its long-range fleet. *Norbert Andrup*

The large fuselage shell of the 747 is ideal for special paint schemes. Airlines around the globe frequently used the Jumbo as a flying advertising column, such as the Lufthansa aircraft seen here. *Gerd Rebenich / Lufthansa*

After the registration D-ABYT was issued to a Lufthansa 747-230M in 1980, the latest version of the Jumbo now also flies with this registration. The 747-8 is finished in a retro scheme, identical to the one in which its forerunner was painted. *Lufthansa*

Lufthansa Boeing 747-8
D-ABYA Brandenburg

LH Deep Blue | C20206 · LH White | R9003 · LH Yellow | C04
LH Light Grey | C01577 · LH Dark Grey | C10002

Left: This color scheme explains the distribution of the predominant blue, white, and gray colors of the current Lufthansa livery on the Boeing 747-8 fleet—including a tiny yellow highlight. *Lufthansa*

Above: The 747-48E(BDSF) with the registration HL7413 is a former passenger Jumbo converted into a freighter by Israel Aerospace Industries. The type designation BDSF stands for BeDek Special Freighter. These conversions can be identified by their extended upper deck, a leftover from their time as passenger aircraft. *Rainer Sonntag*

Above right: Currently operated by Kalitta Air Cargo, this 747-482F(SCD) began its career in 2006 as a Nippon Cargo Airlines freighter with the Japanese registration JA03KZ. *Rainer Sonntag*

Right: Cologne/Bonn airport is a nighttime hub for UPS express freighters. In addition to MD-11Fs, the company also operates this 747-44AF(SCD) with the registration N575UP. *Rainer Sonntag*

therefore met all the existing and planned noise restrictions for commercial aircraft. The new Jumbo also showed itself to be ecologically efficient with regard to fuel consumption. As a "3-liter-aircraft," the 747-8I consumed just 3.5 liters of fuel per passenger per 100 kilometers flown. The Lufthansa flagship also shined when it came to CO_2 emissions, which Boeing had sustainably reduced by 15 percent per passenger compared to the preceding model of the 747 series. The ability of the latest Jumbo generation to present itself as an environmentally friendly aircraft was due not just to its advanced engine technology. The newly developed wing also played a significant part. For example, clear aerodynamic advantages, and therefore lower fuel consumption, were achieved by a new and efficient wing profile and newly developed, so-called raked wingtips. In contrast to the winglets of the earlier aircraft, they were installed horizontally and optimized aerodynamically. Also new was the control of the ailerons and wing spoilers by means of more precise and easier-to-maintain fly-by-wire technology. The latest aluminum alloys with improved resistance to corrosion and weight advantages provided further savings. Progress didn't stop at the cockpit either. The latest generation of the glass cockpit was installed, displaying additional information that enhanced flight safety. Nevertheless, care was taken that the Dash 8's flight deck was largely identical to that of the 747-400, enabling 747-400 simulators to be used to train 747-8I crews. With twenty firm orders and twenty options, Lufthansa was not only launch customer, but also the only purchaser of the passenger version of the 747-8 apart from Korean Air Lines. When delivered, in the Lufthansa layout the airliner was capable of carrying 362 passengers, including eight in first class, ninety-two in business class, and 262 in economy class. Meanwhile a premier economy class was added to the cabin. In contrast to the Boeing 747-400, in which first class was accommodated in the upper deck, Lufthansa placed the premium class in the nose on the main deck of the latest Jumbo Jet generation. Thanks to its special outer-skin insulation, special noise-reducing cabin curtains and footfall insulation, the exclusive first-class cabin is transformed into a quiet feel-good oasis on board the Jumbo.

In 1972 Lufthansa used this advertising photo to show that its 747-230F freighter was capable of carrying seventy-two VW Beetles.
Georg Wegemann / Lufthansa

CONDOR

In April 1970, the management of Condor, then part of the Lufthansa group, announced that it planned to use two Boeing 747-200s to fly to vacation destinations. That was at a time when even renowned carriers such as Pan Am were having difficulty filling the early wide-body jets profitably with passengers. But the West Germans had discovered their love of travel, and the rapidly rising booking numbers for holiday destinations around the Mediterranean—in particular Mallorca—were the precursors of modern-day mass tourism. Compared to the Boeing 727-130s, with 131 seats operated by Condor on its service to Spain, with 470 and later 494 seats, the two 747-230Bs delivered in 1971 and 1972, dubbed Fritz and Max, were true giants.

Condor was not the only one to come up with the idea of offering cheap charter traffic to the warm-water destinations around the Mediterranean. Based in Dusseldorf, LTU began services to Ibiza with its first L-1011-1 on June 14, 1973. While the TriStar carried "just" 359 passengers, Condor and LTU faced the same problem of delivering hundreds of passengers at a time to airports that were then unprepared to receive them. As a creative solution, therefore, Spanish customs agents were on the flight from Germany to Spain, dealing with the arrival formalities while in the air. One day, when both Condor Jumbos landed at Mallorca simultaneously, the customs officials surrendered on the spot to the flood of passengers and quickly opened the airport fence, through which the passengers passed to board shuttle buses waiting to take them to their hotels.

In addition to the relatively short flights to the Mediterranean, the Jumbos were also used on Condor's long-distance routes to Asia and North America. The first two 747-230Bs, with the registrations D-ABYF and D-ABYH, were retired in 1980, but two more Lufthansa aircraft continued flying in Condor colors: 747-230B D-ABYR from January 1979 to May 1980 and 747-430(M) D-ABTD from June 1993 to February 1996. The latter was not used by the charter airline, however. Other airlines established subsidiaries with corresponding cover names, such as Swissair Asia or British Asia Airways, which, pro forma, set them apart from the rest of the fleet.

Condor Boeing 747s were used on flights both to North America and tourist destinations in Asia. This first flight letter documents the start of the connection between Frankfurt and Ceylon—present-day Sri Lanka—in 1971. *Wolfgang Borgmann collection*

After Boeing workers jokingly called the new Condor jet "Big Fritz" during construction, Condor's management decided to adopt this original self-deprecatingly and officially named their first 747-230B Fritz. Outside Germany, this nickname was inspired by Frederick the Great—King of Prussia—who indirectly gave the big Jumbo its name. *Condor*

The two 747-230Bs with the registrations D-ABYF and D-ABYH, which were delivered new by Boeing in 1971 and 1972, were followed by the 747-230M with the registration D-ABYR from the Lufthansa fleet. In contrast to its two predecessors, the third Condor Jumbo was powered by General Electric CF6-50 engines instead of JT9Ds. Condor

Chaotic conditions reigned at airport terminals during the first years of 747 operation, their check-in areas and customs and passport unable to cope with the Jumbo's 470 passengers. Not only as here, on Grand Canary, but also at German airports (for example, Stuttgart), the infrastructure at that time was not set up to handle such masses of people.

BOAC / BRITISH AIRWAYS

In 2019, British Airways celebrated its one hundredth anniversary with special paint schemes on three Boeing 747-400s. On August 25, 1919, the British Aircraft Transport & Travel Limited (AT&T) made its first flight from Hounslow near London to Paris Le Bourget, using an Airco DH.4A bomber converted to carry passengers. This flight is regarded as the birth of British Airways, and while its long and branched family tree reaches back to AT&T, the airline really got going in 1924 with the founding of Imperial Airways under the leadership of the Right Honourable Sir Eric Geddes. Already by 1929, its respectable route network extended to India and by 1934 even to Australia. Although Imperial Airways was established for overseas services, it also maintained contacts with continental Europe, which the British government also regarded as overseas territory. Over these shorter routes in particular, the large and slow Imperial Airways machines had to compete with the faster Lockheed 10 Electras operated by its competitor British Airways, established in 1935. While this predecessor of the modern British Airways had the same name, it was just one of many small airlines, which by order of the British government merged with Imperial Airways to form the British Overseas Airways Corporation (BOAC), officially founded on November 24, 1939. In 1944, together with de Havilland, it began development of the Comet, the first production jet airliner in the world, which on May 2, 1952, launched the "jet age." After British European Airways (BEA) was split off from BOAC on August 1, 1946, it took over its continental European routes and those in the Mediterranean. This split lasted only until 1969, however, when the British government decided to merge BOAC and BEA. After various simulations, this ultimately led on April 1, 1974, to the formation of British Airways. In the coming decades, the BAC/SUD Concorde ordered by BOAC became the flagship of the new British Airways, whose heraldic Speedbird emblem went back to the Imperial Airways of the 1930s. BOAC was also one of the first customers for the Boeing 747-100, with an order for eighteen aircraft, which was issued in stages from 1966 and whose first example was delivered on April 22, 1970—however, because of a strike by BOAC pilots it did not enter service on the British long-range carrier's route network until 1971. The first 747 version was originally supposed to be equipped with the Rolls-Royce RB211 engine; however, Boeing blocked the use of this then completely new type of engine, since Rolls-Royce was unwilling to release technical details about it. Joe Sutter was one of the most vehement critics of the new engine, whose fan blades were made of a composite material called Hyfil in order to save weight. They consisted of a metal shell filled with a mixture of fiberglass and glues. In theory, this material was a quantum leap in engine construction; however, Hyfil failed the required certification tests. Rolls-Royce was forced to completely redesign the engine, which in its revised form as the RB211-524B was to prove to be a reliable and economical engine, and not just on the next 747-236 generation of 747 operated by British Airways.

This 747 pioneering period is recalled by one of the anniversary schemes on its Boeing 747-400 G-BYGC, which is painted in the actual colors worn by BOAC from 1964 to 1974. The aircraft is to retain these colors until it is retired in 2023. The look, created by British design agency Negus & Negus, in which the retro Jumbo is painted with the registration G-CIVB, reflects the original 747 color scheme used by British Airways in 1974.

Boeing 747-400 G-BNLY shines in the elegant Landor design with a blue-gray fuselage and the Speedbird emblem stylized as a red arrow, developed by New York design studio Landor in 1984, and it thus closes the gap to the current Chatham Royal Dockyard design by the British agency Newell & Sorrell, which recalls the flag flown by Admiral Lord Nelson's warship *Victory*, which is based at Chatham Dockyard in London, at the Battle of Trafalgar in 1805.

In the one hundredth year of its long company history, the British airline is a subsidiary of the London-based publicly listed International Airlines Group (IAG),

The British international airline British Overseas Airways Corporation (BOAC) was one of the first customers for the 747-136 and received its first Jumbo with the registration G-AWNA on April 22, 1970. Because of a bitter wage dispute with its pilots, however, the aircraft did not make its first commercial flight until a year later, on April 14, 1971. *British Airways*

which also includes Aer Lingus, the Spanish airline Iberia, and the low-cost airlines Vueling and LEVEL, also Spanish. Founded in 2011, the holding company's estimated 546 aircraft carried almost 113 million passengers in 2018.

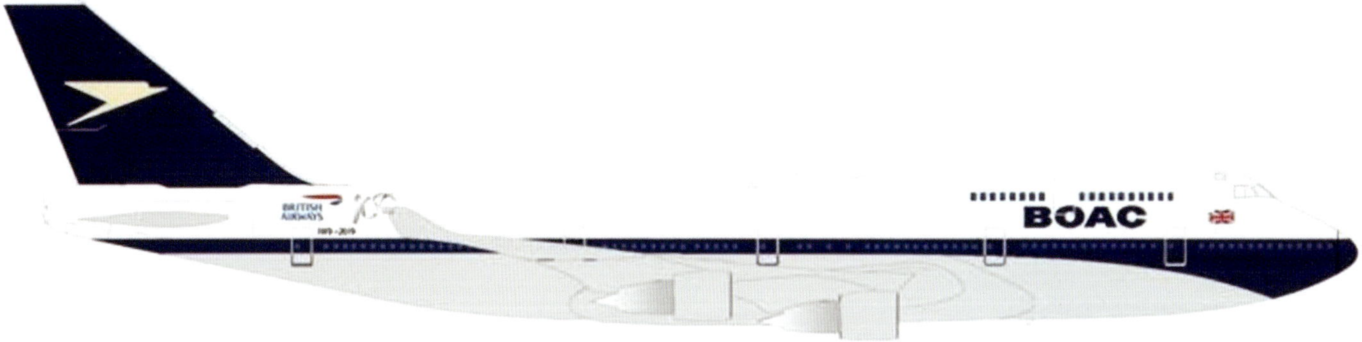

Top of facing page: In the summer of 2019, British Airways proudly unveiled its retro BOAC 747. This livery will remain on the aircraft until its planned retirement in 2023. *British Airways*

Bottom of facing page: The historic 747-136 was the inspiration for one of four retro liveries, which British Airways applied to its 747-436s on the occasion of the airline's one hundredth anniversary. *British Airways*

Above left: The British design firm Negus & Negus designed the first livery for British Airways, formed from BOAC and BEA in 1974, in which the retro Jumbo with the registration G-CIVB is finished.

Above right: Prior to its transformation into a BOAC retro Jumbo, the Boeing 747-436 with the registration G-BYGC taxis to the paint hangar in its initial colors. Introduced in 1997, the Chatham Royal Dockyard livery designed by British agency Newell & Sorrell is based on the flag used by Admiral Nelson in the Battle of Trafalgar in 1805. *British Airways*

Right: The 747-400 G-BNLY gleams in the elegant Landor livery, with a blue-gray fuselage and Speedbird emblem stylized into a red arrow, which was developed by the New York design studio Landor Associates in 1984. *British Airways*

CHAPTER 4
THE SIX BASIC MODELS OF THE JUMBO JET

The Boeing 747-100, deliveries of which began in 1970, was followed in the same year by the improved 747-200B, with an increased maximum takeoff weight of 377 metric tons (415 tons). It quickly became apparent that Joe Sutter and his team had given their Jumbo Jet so much development potential that an entire family of 747 aircraft could emerge from it. No matter if as the 747-200F freighter initiated by Lufthansa, as the short 747SP variant with extremely long range, as the 747-400 with glass cockpit and extended upper deck (also initiated by Lufthansa), as Air Force One used by American presidents, or as the current 747-8 Intercontinental with further developed wings, extremely efficient engines, and lengthened fuselage—the unmistakable Jumbo has become an indispensable part of aviation. The fact also cannot be hidden that not only will the classic 747 of the first two decades soon have disappeared from the skies, but the following further-developed versions will have as well. Only a few 747-400s are still in airline service, and in a few years they will at best still be flying as freighters. With only two customers, it can also be expected of the 747-8 passenger version that in a few years even the most-modern long-range Jumbos will be consigned to "freighter history" or will be directly scrapped.

United Parcel Services (UPS) has operated the Boeing 747 on its worldwide courier and express network since 1984. One of its aircraft was this 747-123(SF), registered N675UP, which was originally delivered new to American Airlines as N9675 in May 1971. Converted into a 747SF with the addition of a side cargo door on the main deck, before it was acquired by UPS the aircraft was operated by Lebanese freight airline TMA before returning to American Airlines for a short time. The Jumbo Jet was scrapped at Roswell, Texas, in 2010. *UPS*

Boeing 747-100	
Wingspan:	195.5 feet
Length:	231.6 feet
Height:	63.3 feet
Wing area:	5,500 square feet
Cabin length:	187 feet
Cabin width:	20 feet
Cabin height:	8.33 feet
Power plant:	4 Pratt & Whitney JT9D-7A
Cruise:	Mach 0.85
Range:	6,089 miles
Cruise altitude:	about 34,449 feet
Cockpit crew:	3

Above left: After delivery of its first three 747-130s, Lufthansa displayed the new fleet flagships at their German stations. D-ABYB, christened Hesse, paid a brief visit to Stuttgart. At that time, the Swabian capital was not a planned destination for Lufthansa's 747s. Seen here, Hesse was the only Lufthansa 747 to be involved in an accident, when on November 20, 1974, under circumstances that remain controversial to this day, after taking off from the Kenyan capital of Nairobi the aircraft descended, struck the runway, and burned out. Fifty-nine of the 157 people on board were killed in the crash. *Lufthansa Photo Archive*

Below left: Air Atlanta Icelandic is a charter airline based in Iceland, which currently has fourteen Boeing 747-400s that it leases to or operates on behalf of other airlines. There are seventy-five Boeing 747-100s and -200s in its historical flight list; however, some of these were only leased from other airlines for a contract lasting several weeks and then moved on from Air Atlanta. The 747-128 TF-ABW shown here was originally built for Air France, while the Nigerian operator Kabo Air, Avianca of Colombia, Air Club International of Canada, and Iberia of Spain all leased the aircraft from Air Atlanta Icelandic for a time. *Wolfgang Borgmann collection*

Right: On the occasion of the official rollout of the 747 prototype, Boeing invited a stewardess from each of the first customers to the christening of the Jumbo Jet. At the command of the speaker giving the laudation, each of the stewardesses was supposed to break a bottle of champagne against the jet. Some of the stewardesses misunderstood their instructions, however, and broke their bottle of champagne either too soon or too late. To the amusement of those present, the christening of the City of Everett descended into champagne chaos. To illustrate the size of the Jumbo's JT9D engines, each customer had a photo taken of one of its stewardesses sitting on the nacelle. In the photo below is a stewardess of the Scandinavian airline SAS, which had ordered two 747-200Bs. *SAS*

Boeing 747-200	
Wingspan:	195.5 feet
Length:	231.6 feet
Height:	63.3 feet
Wing area:	5,500 square feet
Cabin length:	187 feet
Cabin width:	20 feet
Cabin height:	8.33 feet
Power plants:	4 Pratt & Whitney JT9D-7R
	General Electric CF-6
	Rolls-Royce RB211
Cruise:	Mach 0.85
Range:	6,089 miles
Cruise altitude:	about 34,449 feet
Cockpit crew:	3

Above left: Air France was one of the very first customers for the Boeing 747. Its first example was the nineteenth Jumbo built, which the airline flew to France on March 20, 1970, bearing the registration F-BPVA. Like Lufthansa, Air France ordered a single 747-228F freighter with Pratt & Whitney engines; however, all of its other freighters had General Electric CF-6 engines (see photo). Air France retired its last Jumbo—a 747-428 passenger aircraft—in January 2016. *Air France*

Below left: Spirit of Hong Kong 97 is the name of this special livery, in which Cathay Pacific's 747-267B with the registration B-HIB was finished on the occasion of the return of the former British colony to the People's Republic of China in 1997. It depicts the high-rise silhouette of the economic metropolis. *Wolfgang Borgmann collection*

Facing page: With 114 Boeing 747s, Japan Air was the biggest purchaser of the wide-body jet. They included this 747-200F(SCD) with the registration JA8123, which was delivered to JAL in September 1974. In April 2002, it was sold to its second and last owner, the American-owned Kalitta Air Cargo, which finally decommissioned the aircraft on Christmas Eve 2008. *Wolfgang Borgmann collection*

JAL CARGO
JAL

With nineteen 747-200Fs, Flying Tiger once operated the biggest all-freighter fleet of Boeing 747s in the world. *Wolfgang Borgmann collection*

After the purchase of Flying Tiger by the express cargo company Federal Express on January 29, 1989, some of the former Flying Tiger 747s continued flying in the new FedEx colors until 1999. *Wolfgang Borgmann collection*

Above left: SAS 747-238 B Huge Viking photographed during takeoff. Visible in the background are the gigantic final-assembly hangar for the Jumbo Jet and the summit of Mount Rainier near Seattle. *SAS*

Below left: For a short time between March 1986 and November 1988, Air India Cargo leased this 747-200F, which Boeing had delivered to World Airways in April 1973. In its eventful service life, the jumbo freighter also flew for Air Algerie, Flying Tiger Line, Malaysia Airlines, National Airlines, Pan Am, Saudi Arabian Airlines VIASA, and finally, until its retirement in December 2012, Evergreen International Airlines. *Wolfgang Borgmann collection*

Above: When Boeing released this brochure in the 1980s, the 747 had no competitors in its size class. *Boeing*

Above: KLM, SAS, Swissair, and UTA formed the KSSU alliance solely for the purpose of providing technical support for their small 747 fleets. KLM assumed responsibility for overhauling its partners' Jumbos, while UTA in Paris maintained the auxiliary power units in the tail of the aircraft, and SAS the aircraft's JT9D engines in Stockholm. *KLM*

Right: Dan Viking—a 747-283M Combi operated by SAS—was the five hundredth Jumbo Jet delivered by Boeing. SAS received the aircraft, with the registration N4501Q, in February 1981. *Boeing*

What looks like a playroom was actually the planning office in which SAS made preparations for the ground handling of the 747 in the late 1960s. The unprecedented size of the Jumbo, which entered service in 1970, required detailed concepts, such as the optimal sequence in which servicing vehicles should be placed around the aircraft. Nowadays such planning is carried out on a computer, but in those analog times, this was the best way of simulating a servicing process and identifying potential weaknesses in advance. Such large models, which are now treasured collectors' items, were used not only by SAS but by most 747 customers around the globe. *SAS*

Final assembly of the first of two 747-200Cs, combined passenger-freight versions, destined for Martinair Holland. They were delivered in February 1987 and could be operated as pure freighters or as combined passenger-freight aircraft. In contrast to the 747-200M, which was operated as a combi, the 747-200C had a nose cargo door in addition to the big side cargo door in the aft fuselage. *Boeing*

This cutaway drawing shows the possible cabin arrangement of a 747-200M Combi. The combis with the large cargo door in the aft fuselage but without the nose cargo door were very popular with airlines in the 1980s. Only by carrying profitable airfreight could some air routes be served economically by a wide-body jet. The increased passenger and freight traffic of the present day, however, makes it necessary to operate pure passenger aircraft and dedicated freighters. Nevertheless, the air cargo carried in the underfloor cargo holds of the 747-400 and 747-8 makes a significant contribution to a route's viability. *Boeing*

Meeting of Jumbos at Terminal 1 of the Paris Charles de Gaulle airport in the 1990s. *Left*: a Boeing 747-400 of Japan Air Lines; *right*: a 747-200 of Air France.
Wolfgang Borgmann collection

This Boeing 747SP was the one and only Jumbo Jet flown by Kazakhstan Airlines. The aircraft was originally delivered to TWA in April 1980, and after a stopover at American Airlines, in February 1994 it went to the airline of the former Soviet republic, which since December 16, 1991, has been an independent state. *Rainer Sonntag*

Boeing 747SP	
Wingspan:	195.5 feet
Length:	184.7 feet
Height:	65.4 feet
Wing area:	5,500 square feet
Cabin length:	137.8 feet
Cabin width:	20 feet
Cabin height:	8.3 feet
Power plants:	4 Pratt & Whitney JT9D-7R / Rolls-Royce RB211
Cruise:	Mach 0.90
Range:	9,569 miles
Cruise altitude:	about 44,947 feet
Cockpit crew:	3

Boeing 747-300	
Wingspan:	195.5 feet
Length:	231.6 feet
Height:	63.3 feet
Wing area:	5,500 square feet
Cabin length:	187 feet
Cabin width:	20 feet
Cabin height:	8.3 feet
Power plants:	4 Pratt & Whitney JT9D-7R / General Electric CF-6 /
	Rolls-Royce RB211
Cruise:	Mach 0.85
Range:	7,705 miles
Cruise altitude:	about 34,449 feet
Cockpit crew:	3

Above right: In addition to brand-new 747-300s, Boeing offered to convert existing 747-200Bs with the lengthened upper deck, which were initially marketed as the 747-200 Stretched Upper Deck (SUD). KLM took advantage of this offer and had ten aircraft converted by its technical department in Amsterdam, while UTA of France converted two of its 747-200Bs in Paris. As well, Japan Air Lines had Boeing convert two brand-new aircraft into the 747-100B/SUD version with the lengthened upper deck prior to their acceptance. *Swissair, ETH-Bibliothek, Zurich*

Right: The 747-300 was not very popular with the airlines, since while it could carry more passengers, it brought no technological advancements compared to the 747-200B. Maximum takeoff weight remained unchanged, and with the greater structural weight of the lengthened upper deck, this resulted in a reduction in range. *Wolfgang Borgmann collection*

Above: Swissair was the first customer for the 747-300, placing an order for four aircraft on June 11, 1980, later augmented by a further example. The first Jumbo with the lengthened upper deck was not delivered to the Swiss airline, however, instead going to the French airline UTA. Apart from the upper deck, which was lengthened by about 23 feet and accommodated up to sixty-nine passengers, outwardly the 747-300 was no different from the two preceding versions. Of the eighty-one examples built, fifty-six were pure passenger versions and twenty-one were combis with a side cargo door. Four days after UTA, Swissair received its first 747-300 and on March 23, 1983, it became the first airline to use this variant on a scheduled service. Just four examples of the 747-300SR short-range version were made, and all went to Japan Air Lines for use on Japanese domestic routes. With a maximum range of just 2,361 miles, the 747-300SR was capable of carrying a maximum of 624 passengers. *Swissair, ETH-Bibliothek, Zurich*

Left: It was more comfortable on board a Swissair aircraft than on the Japanese 747-300SR domestic version. When business class was first introduced in March 1984, their 747-300s were equipped with thirty-six "slumberette" seats in first class, sixty-three seats in business class, and 276 seats in economy—sixty-nine of them in the lengthened upper deck. *Swissair, ETH-Bibliothek, Zurich*

The 747-400 was built in greater numbers than any other version of the wide-body jet, with 694 examples completed. *Boeing*

Boeing 747-400	
Wingspan:	211.4 feet
Length:	231.6 feet
Height:	63.7 feet
Wing area:	5,825 square feet
Cabin length:	187 feet
Cabin width:	20 feet
Cabin height:	8.3 feet
Power plants:	4 General Electric CF6-80 / Pratt & Whitney PW 4062 / Rolls-Royce RB211-524
Cruise:	Mach 0.85
Range:	about 6,835 miles
Cruise altitude:	ca. 34,449 feet
Cockpit crew:	2

The figures for range and altitude are approximate values, which depend on payload and fuel quantity as well meteorological conditions of each flight.

Above left: Based in Calgary, Canadian Airlines International became the second-largest Canadian airline after the merger of CPAir, Nordair, and Pacific Western in 1987. In addition to McDonnell Douglas DC-10s and Boeing 767s, it operated Boeing 747-400s, mainly on its international routes. After financial difficulties, in 1999 Air Canada acquired the majority of shares in its biggest competitor, which by 2001 was completely integrated into the country's largest airline. *Wolfgang Borgmann collection*

Below left: Japan Air Lines was one of the biggest Asian customers for the Boeing 747, and in addition to the 747-400 version shown here, it also flew the 747-100, -200, and -300 in a variety of versions as passenger aircraft and freighters. *Boeing*

Opposite: When Air Namibia acquired a Boeing 747-400M Combi with the registration V5-NMA in 1999, its capacity quickly proved too large. It was soon replaced by two McDonnell Douglas MD-11s; however, these also proved to be too large and were in turn replaced by two A340-300s. *Boeing*

Air Namibia
BOEING 747-400
WELWITSCHIA
The National Airline of Namibia

Above left: The Lufthansa Technik workshops in Hamburg specialized in equipping VIP cabins, such as that of this 747-400 of the Sultan of Oman seen here. *Lufthansa Technik*

Left: In 2016 the standard Lufthansa 747-400 Potsdam became the "Fanhansa Siegerflieger." It flew the victorious German Football Association team, which had just won the World Cup, from Brazil back to Berlin. *Lufthansa*

Above right: Not shrunken 747 tails, but the winglets, which, mounted on the wingtips, reduce drag and thus fuel consumption; these were painted in the colors of the various customers. *Boeing*

Opposite: Taken in October 1993, this photo depicts the final assembly steps on the first 747-400F freighter destined for Cargolux at the Boeing factory in Everett. The airline from Luxembourg was the first customer for the then-newest Jumbo freighter. At that time, Air France, Asiana, Cathay Pacific, KLM, and Singapore Airlines were already on the customer list for the 747-400F. *Boeing*

st Boeing
0 Freighter for
cargolux

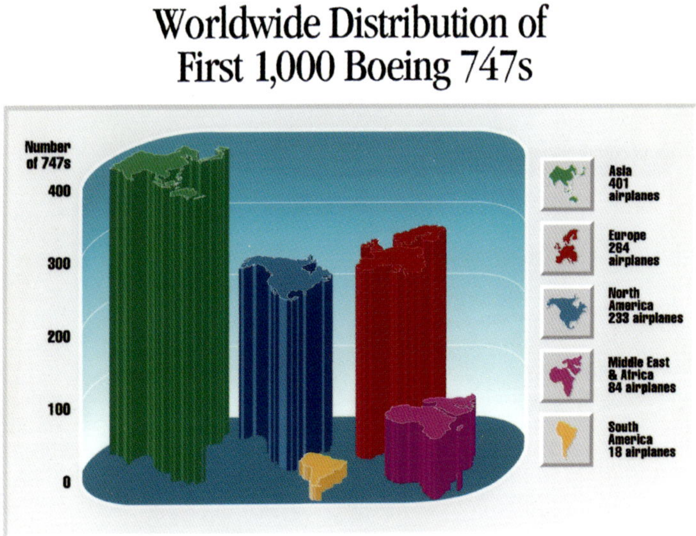

Above left: Besides British Airways, Virgin Atlantic—one of its fiercest competitors in the British domestic market—was also a longtime customer of the Boeing 747 series. These included the 747-4Q8 with the registration G-VTOP, which after it was retired by Virgin finished its career with Orient Thai Airlines, based in Bangkok. *Boeing*

Left: The 747-400ERF seen here is one of forty of the freighter version of the Extended Range ultra-long-range version of the 747-400. Jade cargo was a joint venture among Lufthansa Cargo (25%), the Deutsche Entwicklungsgesellschaft (24%), and Shenzhen Airlines (51%). As the first Chinese freight airline with foreign participation, it began operations in August 2006. The six 747-400ERF transports had to be decommissioned in 2011 due to lack of interest. The following year the German-Chinese cooperative project was finally buried. *Jim Anderson / Lufthansa*

Above right: In September 1993 Boeing published this graphic showing the worldwide distribution of the one thousand 747s sold to date. At that time, 108 customers in fifty-one countries were flying Jumbos. About 89 percent of the Boeing 747s built were delivered to airlines based outside the United States, and 95 percent of all 747-400s sold were exported. Adjusted for the effects of inflation, by then Boeing had earned a whopping 141.8 billion US dollars from all the 747s it had sold—including $115 billion from sales to foreign customers. *Boeing*

Roughly a quarter of a century separates the development of the 747-400's glass cockpit (*left*) and that of the 747-100 basic model (*right*), shown here for comparison. Boeing achieved this quantum leap only under pressure from several airlines, which insisted on a radical adaptation of the 747-400 cockpit to the then-most-advanced technologies. *Boeing*

Above left: This photo shows the large size of the area between the aircraft's outer skin and the cabin roof, which is otherwise not visible to passengers. Supply lines run through this area; for example, the air-conditioning system (*center of photo*) and the control cables between the cockpit and the control surfaces (*top*). Passenger seats can be seen at the bottom left. *Lufthansa Technik*

Left: The aircraft in this photo, still in passenger service with the South Korean airline Asiana, has since been converted into a 747-48E(BDSF) freighter and is now operated by Asiana Cargo. *Boeing*

Above right: Ready for a fresh load of airfreight. *Boeing*

Opposite, above: This 747-UF(SCD) of the British cargo airline Global Supply Systems was photographed on the ramp at Munich airport. The company flew exclusively for British Airways World Cargo and last operated three 747-8Fs on its behalf and in its livery. In 2014, British Airways terminated the lease early. Unable to find a new customer, Global Supply Systems ceased operations later that year. *Wolfgang Borgmann collection*

Opposite, below: Quantas was the first airline in the world to order the longer-range version of the 747-400, which became the 747-400ER. The Australian airline, which took delivery of the first of six examples on October 31, 2002, was not only the first but also the only customer for this jet, which was tailored to its needs. The final example was handed over to Quantas on July 30, 2003. *Boeing*

Global Supply Systems
G-GSSB

QANTAS
THE AUSTRALIAN AIRLINE

Lufthansa
D-ABYA

Boeing 747-8	
Wingspan:	224.4 feet
Length:	250.3 feet
Height:	63.6 feet
Wing area:	5,963 square feet
Cabin length:	187 feet
Cabin width:	20 feet
Cabin height:	8.3 feet
Power plant:	4 GEnx-2B67
Cruise:	Mach 0.855
Range:	about 9,196 miles
Cruise altitude:	about 34,449 feet
Cockpit crew:	2

Opposite: Lufthansa 747-8 in the airline's new look. Lufthansa originally ordered twenty aircraft; however, it received just nineteen. *Lufthansa*

Right: In contrast to those of the 747-400, the further-developed wings of the 747-8 (*top photo*) have so-called raked wingtips, which in principle have the same drag-reducing function as the vertical winglets (*bottom*) of its predecessor, but being horizontal they increase the wingspan of the 747-8. *Boeing*

Above left: Thanks to its four General Electric GEnx-2B engines adopted from the Boeing 787, which are its exclusive power plants, the 747-8 is one-third quieter during takeoff than the 747-400. Compared to the earlier model, CO_2 emissions have also dropped by a considerable 15 percent per passenger. As a so-called 3-liter aircraft, the 747-8I burns 0.9 US gallons of jet fuel per passenger per 62 miles flown. *Lufthansa*

Left: Final assembly of the first 747-8 destined for Lufthansa. The German airline, Air China, and Korean Air Lines are the only airlines in the world to have ordered a passenger version. *Boeing*

Opposite: Korean Air Lines operates eleven 747-8B5s in a pure passenger configuration and six 747-8B5F freighters. *Rainer Sonntag*

KOREAN AIR
대한항공

KOREAN AIR CARGO
대한항공

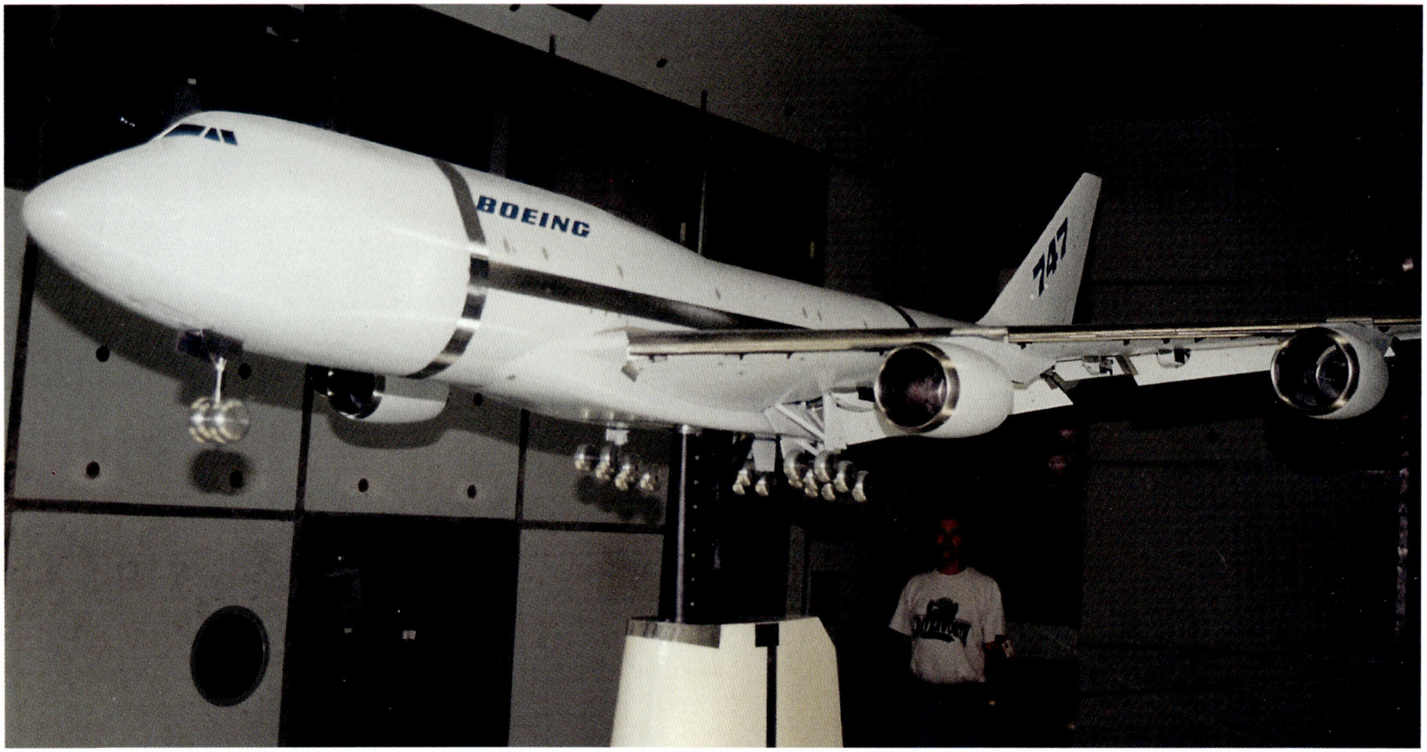

Planning for the 747-500X and -600X had progressed so far that Boeing had already tested large models in the wind tunnel to obtain reliable data about their expected flight characteristics and performance parameters. *Boeing*

Opposite: After the launch of the 747-400, Boeing planned an entire family of wide-body jets with even-greater range and payload. Neither the 747-500X nor 747-600X was able to generate enthusiasm among the airlines, however, and so the designs disappeared back into the drawers of the aircraft maker's development department. *Boeing*

747-500X/-600X

THE JUMBO JETS THAT WERE NEVER BUILT

Alarmed by the Airbus announcement that it planned to build the A-3XX project, a passenger aircraft even larger than the 747-400, Boeing planned a suitable answer to the challenge from Toulouse with the 747-500X and the -600X. Powered by fuel-saving Engine Alliance GP 7100 or Rolls-Royce Trent turbofan engines, with a modern fly-by-wire flight control system the 747-500X would be capable of carrying 462 passengers in a three-class version over 9,942 miles, while the further-lengthened 747-600X would be able to carry about 547 passengers over 8,917 miles. As Boeing announced in a press report in November 1996, at that time the manufacturer was working with nineteen airlines on development of the newest member of the 747 family. In the end, however, the concept failed to convince any of the potential customers, who at that point in time gave preference to an entirely new design in the shape of the A380 over a "warmed-up" 747.

747
BOEING 747-400
747
BOEING 747-500X
747
BOEING 747-600X

CHAPTER 5
ON BOARD THE BOEING 747

THE JUMBO FEELING

Traveling on a Boeing 747 has been a unique flight experience since the first flight of a Pan Am aircraft in 1970. No other jet offers such a spatial experience and space as a Jumbo Jet—even in economy class, where at times the distances between seats are extremely tight. In contrast, when the 747 was first introduced, the airlines were able to compete only on the service offered and not on the price, since air fares set by the cartel of the International Aviation Organization were binding for all airlines. It is not surprising, therefore, that the early customers of the Jumbo Jet outbid each other with the space offered on their jets and the exquisite food and spirits on offer. Moreover, the 747 was completely oversized for most markets in the early 1970s. The oil crisis of the early seventies, in particular, resulted in almost empty cabins in which the few passengers became accustomed to a level of comfort that remains to be matched in 2019. If one looks at the historical seating plans of Jumbo Jet cabins, one sees that in place of today's economy-class seating, with ten seats per row, only nine seats were installed. As a result, not only were the seats significantly wider, the distance between rows was also more generous than usual nowadays. A Boeing 747-200 of Scandinavian Airlines or one of its then identically configured partner Swissair had 353 seats at the time it entered service in 1972. Ten years later, equipped with ten seats per row, the maximum number of seats on board the SAS 747B was 396. In the 1970s, no airlines offered a business class or upgraded premium economy class on long-range flights. Instead, economy-class passengers received a level of service that does not need to shy away from comparison with the upgraded travel classes of the present. The ultimate luxury was offered by American Airlines on board its 747 Astro Jet fleet: a lounge above the clouds with a comfortable sofa landscape and piano bar—all of this, mind you, for economy-class passengers. In first class the passengers could reserve tables for three or four persons on the main deck and there take their exquisite meals or hold a business meeting.

The legendary Pan Am bar service is part of the special experience that is the Pan Am Experience located at the gates of Los Angeles. Dishes prepared according to original recipes of the Pan Am catering department during the simulated journey allow one to feel what a flight on a Pan Am Boeing 747-121 in the 1970s was like. *Pan Am Experience*

The area behind the cockpit was reserved for a first-class lounge by all early 747 customers. Its seats could not be reserved; instead they were accessible by the passengers seated below in first class after the seat belt sign was switched off. The upper deck of the first three 747 versions was reached by a spiral staircase, which was a homage to the Boeing 377 Stratocruiser of the 1940s, whose cocktail bar was also reached by a spiral staircase from the main deck. While most airlines spoiled their passengers with mainly alcoholic drinks and small snacks, Pan Am's upper-deck lounge served as a flying restaurant. Passengers traveling in first class were asked, when they selected their choices from the menu at the latest, whether they would like to eat it in their seat in the President Class section in the nose of the 747—or at the two- or four-seat tables in the upper deck. Pan Am thus transformed its 747 Clippers into temporary restaurants with the most breathtaking view of their time.

And something else that made traveling on a 747 different than present-day flight experiences: compared to today, the passengers were elegantly dressed. While flying has by now become a mass phenomenon and even first- and business-class passengers travel in shorts and sneakers, this was unimaginable in the 1970s. Instead, gentlemen on long-distance flights preferred a suit and tie, and ladies wore elegant clothes—no matter the class in which they were flying. It is thanks to Antony Toth's enthusiasm for the Boeing 747 and Pan Am that one can relive this flight experience from a long-past era of air travel. It sounds like a cliché, but it was in his garage in Redondo Beach, California, that Anthony Toth first built the first-class nose section of a Pan Am 747-221, which he equipped with original interior furnishings and catering items, magazines, safety cards, food carts, and onboard tableware from the estate of Pan Am—to peanut bags and cocktail sticks. Even the fabric Clipper motif that adorned the wardrobe doors in the nose is an original. Toth had other cabin details, such as a glass room divider on the upper deck, made on the basis of historical photos. What was originally intended as an unusual hobby and a meeting place with friends quickly developed into an increasingly large project, which after two moves and modifications now consists of a business-class section and the original first-class upper deck of a Pan Am 747-221 from the 1970s. Meanwhile, the time machine based in Los Angeles takes off regularly on commercially bookable sightseeing flights, the only goal of which is to re-create the flight experience of that time as authentically as possible. The passengers, all elegantly dressed, are welcomed on board the Pan Am Experience 747 in Pacoima by crew members dressed in historical Pan Am uniforms and are served from a menu, depending on class, based on original Pan Am catering recipes. According to Pan Am Experience, there have been no empty seats since the "maiden flight" of the Clipper Juan Trippe on October 18, 2014. The passenger list ranges from former Pan Am staff and passengers to aviation enthusiasts and fans of the 1970s lifestyle.

The gradual liberalization of global air traffic, which began in the United States in 1978 with the Airline Deregulation Act by the US administration under Jimmy Carter, meant the irretrievable end of the luxury era on board the Boeing 747. Even the small upper decks of the 747-100 and -200 were now filled with revenue-generating economy-class seats in place of first-class lounges, while as many as ninety-nine economy seats—equal to the capacity of a regional jet—now occupied the lengthened upper deck of the 747-300. If one compares the configuration of the few Boeing 747-400s and 747-8s still used in long-distance passenger traffic today, their cabin layout does not differ one bit from that of other long-range types. The era of flying lounges is finally a thing of the past.

Above: In the 1970s the upper deck of most Boeing 747-100s and -200s was reserved as an exclusive lounge for first-class passengers. *Pan Am Experience*

Above right: Each airline chose a different layout of its lounge in the 747's upper deck. While Pan Am used this area as a flying restaurant and therefore installed more seats and tables, SAS chose a more generous seat landscape. *SAS*

Right: Prior to the modern smoking ban, enjoying a good cigar in the first-class lounge after an opulent meal above the clouds was a pleasant travel experience for many passengers. *Swissair, ETH-Bibliothek, Zurich*

Above: This advertisement from the 1970s is not promoting a lounge in first class, but rather the one in economy class on board an American Airlines Boeing 747. Current economy-class passengers can only dream of such luxury. *Wolfgang Borgmann collection*

Above left: In 1970, Lufthansa spoiled its economy-class passengers on long-range flights on the Boeing 747-130 with relatively generous leg spacing and dishes served from the serving trolley on porcelain plates. *Lufthansa Photo Archive / Lufthansa*

Left: In 1979, Lufthansa became one of the first airlines in the world to introduce a business class on long-range flights. The well-upholstered seats were arranged in a 2-3-2 configuration; however, it did not come close to the space offered today. *Fritz Dressler / Lufthansa*

This photo is from the 1990s. It shows first class, then the top product offered by Lufthansa on board the 747-400. *Wolfgang Fritz / Lufthansa*

Above left: From 1998, Lufthansa's first-class passengers sat in these seats, which were designed by Frog Design and inspired by the corrugated-metal fuselage of the Ju 52/3m, and not just in the 747 upper deck shown here. *M. Schulze-Alex / Lufthansa Technik AG*

Left: In the last-offered generation of Lufthansa first class, in addition to the actual seat there is a bed, which is especially popular on night flights. *Lufthansa*

Opposite: In addition to first class, business class, and economy class, many airlines also offer a somewhat better eco class. It complies with the requirements of the companies' travel agencies, which allow their employees a long-haul flight only in economy class. *Lufthansa*

Today's generation of business-class seats can be electronically extended to create horizontal beds, as seen here in the upper deck of a Lufthansa Boeing 747-400. Lufthansa

The ultimate travel experience on board a Lufthansa jet is offered by first class installed in the nose sections of its 747-8s. Special insulation makes this exclusive area the quietest area on the latest generation of the Jumbo Jet. Lufthansa

CHAPTER 6 SPECIAL-VERSION JUMBOS

In addition to its traditional role as passenger, VIP, and freight aircraft, special versions of the Boeing 747 are operated by the armed forces, on behalf of the space agency NASA, as special transports and as water bombers around the globe. Here is a selection of the most-spectacular projects.

BOEING 747-24GB (VC-25A): AIR FORCE ONE; THE US PRESIDENTIAL AIRCRAFT

Of all the VIP jets used by global heads of state and government leaders, a special aura surrounds Air Force One, on which the president of the United States travels. The tradition of selecting certain transport aircraft for air travel by the US president began in the 1930s, but the Douglas C-54 Sacred Cow was reserved exclusively for Franklin D. Roosevelt in 1944 and was equipped with an elevator for the thirty-second president of the United States, who was confined to a wheelchair. While Harry S. Truman entrusted himself to a Douglas C-118 Liftmaster, Dwight D. Eisenhower from November 1952 until November 1954 exclusively used the VC-121A Constellation named Columbine II for his travels. It was followed by the VC-121E Super Constellation with the name Columbine III and the serial 53-7885, until in 1960 presidential travel entered the jet age with the Boeing 707 (VC-137B) Special Air Mission (SAM) 970.

Since 1990, the president of the United States has flown in one of the two VC-25A aircraft available to them. The two aircraft, based on the 747-200 and with the serials 92-9000 and 82-8000, are completely identical in appearance and sit parked side by side ready to fly when the president leaves on a trip. For security reasons, it is not decided until immediately prior to departure on which of the two aircraft the president will actually fly—and which of the two aircraft will officially become Air Force One. If the president is not

From a distance, the Boeing 747-2G4B (VC-25A) is hardly distinguishable from an airline version of the 747-200B. *US government*

on board one of the two aircraft, its call sign changes either to SAM 28000 or SAM 29000. That the call sign can also change during flight in Air Force One was shown during the transport of the assassinated president John F. Kennedy from Dallas to Washington, DC, on November 22, 1963. The flight took off as SAM 2600; however, after the swearing in of Vice President Lyndon B. Johnson as the new American president, it landed in the American capital as Air Force One. Should an American president travel in an aircraft or helicopter of the US Army, Navy, or Coast Guard, that flight, analogous to with the Air Force jets, is given the call sign Army One, Navy One, Marine One, or Coast Guard One.

The interior design of the VC-25A is, like a flying White House, conceived as the office of the president. On board there is a communications center, briefing rooms, medical care, a kitchen, an area for security personnel traveling with the president and government guests and representatives of the press—and of course the president's office. The days of the two current presidential aircraft are numbered, however, since the conversion of one of two 747-85Ms, which were purchased secondhand, into VC-25Bs at Boeing's Texas factory in San Antonio has already begun. Interestingly, the two jets that have been selected were originally ordered by the Russian airline Transaero, which became insolvent in 2015, and the aircraft were initially mothballed at an aircraft storage site in Victorville, California. Including all the follow-up costs, the procurement of the two VC-25Bs will cost the United States more than five billion dollars.

Above: Former president Obama and members of the Presidential Logistics Squadron (PLS) pose for a group photo in front of Air Force One on May 4, 2015. The PLS is responsible for maintaining the VC-25A. *US Air Force / SMSgt. Kevin Wallace*

Left: If the US president is traveling, for security reasons he does not decide until shortly before departure which of the two identical VC-25As parked side by side on the ramp he will use. Only then does it become Air Force One. *US Air Force / SMSgt. Kevin Wallace*

In this symbolic picture, the aircraft of the current American president flies over his predecessors George Washington, Thomas Jefferson, Theodore Roosevelt, and Abraham Lincoln, carved in stone on Mount Rushmore in South Dakota. *US Air Force*

This artwork illustrates the operating principle of the YAL-1A Airborne Laser, based on a Boeing 747-400F, whose infrared beam heats the outer skin of an incoming ballistic missile, which is supposed to cause them to melt. *US Air Force*

YAL-1A AIRBORNE LASER: STAR WARS

It sounds like an episode from the motion picture *Star Wars*, in which the combatants are fighting with light sabers—but the YAL-1A, which was built at the turn of the twenty-first century and tested until 2012, was a real laser weapon based on the Boeing 747-400F. A high-energy laser beam was generated in its cargo hold, which was directed at hostile targets by a firing mechanism in the nose. A technique was used in which a chemical reaction generated energy that was released, converted into light, and bundled into a laser beam. The idea of shooting down enemy missiles with lasers was not new. In the 1980s, using the NKC-135A Laser Lab, the US Air Force developed a specialized system for destroying air-to-air missiles from short range, which was installed in a modified Boeing 717 (KC-135). Conversely, the YAL-1A Airborne Laser transmits invisible rays in the infrared range, which initially caused no obvious damage to the object to be destroyed. Instead, the object was to heat the outer metal skin of the ballistic missile immediately after launch, causing it to become unstable, whereupon the missile—like the pouring of molten lead on New Year's Eve—lost its shape and crashed. Whether the first high-energy shot fired by the YAL-1A on February 11, 2010, was successful has not been made public. In any case, the costs do not seem to have been in proportion to the result. Of the seven planned weapons systems, just one test aircraft was built, which in 2012 was mothballed at the US Air Force boneyard near Tucson, Arizona. In addition to Boeing, Northrop Grumman and Lockheed Martin also took part in the project, contributing the laser and the fire control system. Reactivation of the YAL-1A is theoretically possible, should the American military decide to revive the Airborne Laser Project.

It looks like an episode from the epic movie Star Wars—but the YAL-1A, which is equipped with a laser for shooting down enemy missiles, was reality and was supposed to pave the way to a completely new laser weapons system. *United States Missile Defense Agency*

BOEING 747SP-21: N747NA IN THE SERVICE OF SCIENCE

SOFIA, the only space telescope installed in an aircraft anywhere in the world, was jointly employed by the American space agency NASA and the German Center for Air and Space Travel (DLR) to explore space. SOFIA stands for Stratospheric Observatory for Infrared Astronomy, and it permits the exploration of our solar system and distant galaxies particularly well, since the 747SP flies at an altitude of up to 45,932 feet—and is thus above 99 percent of the earth's atmosphere, which blocks infrared rays. SOFIA thus provided American and German astronomers with fascinating views of space that would not be possible with conventional infrared telescopes from the earth's surface. The flying platform was a Boeing 747SP-21, which was delivered new to Pan Am on May 6, 1977, with the registration N536PA. In the old Pan Am tradition the aircraft was initially given a Clipper name. In this case, Anne Morrow Lindbergh, widow of the legendary airman Charles Lindbergh, was the naming patron. On the fiftieth anniversary of the first solo flight across the North Atlantic by her husband, who had died in 1974, Boeing named the aircraft Clipper Lindbergh in his memory. The choice of name was also an homage by the airline to Lindbergh's role in the establishment of new Pan Am routes in the postwar period, on which, as a member of Pan Am's board of directors and personal advisor to company founder Juan Trippe, he had considerable influence. Despite his fame, not only in aviation circles, Charles Lindbergh was a reserved and humble person. On his many business trips with Pan Am, he always flew anonymously and exclusively in economy class.

After the sale of the Clipper Lindbergh to United Airlines in 1986, until 1994 the United operated the SP primarily on its Pacific routes. Two years later, NASA purchased the aircraft, by then parked in an aircraft boneyard, and in 1999 began converting it into a flying observatory. The Boeing 747SP had to be completely reworked for its role as a flying observatory, not just to accommodate the telescope cabin but also the workstations for the up to fifteen scientists and technicians in the passenger cabin in front of it. The greatest challenge, however, was the installation of an opening in the fuselage through which the telescope looked into space. The complex task was carried out by the specialists of L3 Communications Integrated Systems in Waco, Texas. Its engineers thought it safer to initially modify an original fuselage section 46 from a scrapped United 747SP with a new pressure bulkhead, the large telescope door, and a mockup of the telescope, so that, using this full-scale model, it could test the feasibility of a conversion of a Jumbo Jet, which had never before been attempted. The installation of the telescope, and especially of the door, which would be opened at near the speed of sound, required a significant change in the original aircraft structure. At the end of 1999, the full-scale model of the telescope was ready to be placed in the test fuselage. Building on this experience, the team went to work on the real aircraft and the tricky conversion. In September 2002, the telescope, which had been made in Germany, arrived in Waco on board an Airbus A300-600ST Beluga, disassembled into telescope frame, mounting, and primary mirror for transport. Together with the employees of the German SOFIA Institute and the DLR, who had also traveled from Germany, specialists of L-3 Communications Integrated Systems integrated the valuable object into the modified aircraft structure. After the extensive conversion, including the pressure bulkhead fitted between the passenger cabin and telescope, in April 2007 the first test flight was made with the telescope door closed. Not until December 18, 2009, had the certification flights and ground tests advanced so far that for the first time the 14.75-foot telescope door was opened in flight.

The centerpiece of the system was the 22-ton, 106-inch telescope made by high-tech-companies of Germany, with an effective usable diameter of 100 inches, which, thanks to the great range of the 747SP, was used around the globe. The SOFIA telescope was developed and produced on behalf of the DLR, primarily by MT Aerospace AG and the

With its onboard infrared telescope, SOFIA (Stratospheric Observatory for Infrared Astronomy), a modified Boeing 747SP, was used for exploration of our solar system and distant galaxies. At an altitude of up to 45,932 feet, SOFIA operated above 99 percent of the earth's infrared-blocking atmosphere and thus enabled images that would not be possible from the ground in this quality. *NASA*

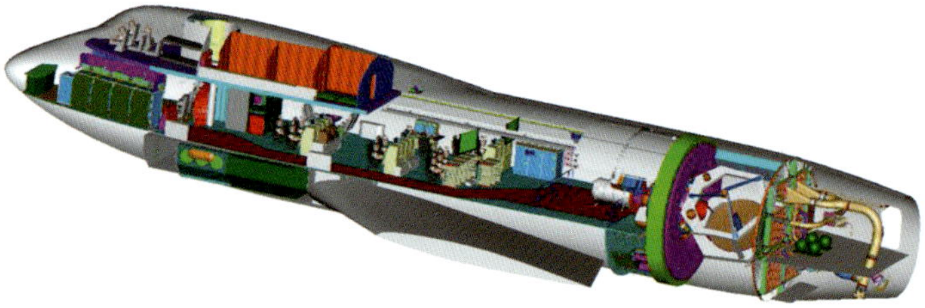

Kayser-Threde GmbH, with the participation of numerous European subcontractors. SOFIA explored the infrared universe, since many objects in space radiate almost all of their energy in the infrared wavelength and not as light. If a telescope is pointed at them, they remain invisible to the human eye. This is also true of interstellar objects, whose visible light is shielded by clouds of gas and dust in space, which is no obstacle for infrared radiation. During the approximately ten-hour observation flights, the telescope was used to investigate the births and deaths of stars, the formation of new solar systems and mysterious black holes in the midst of galaxies.

Compared to research satellites in earth orbit, SOFIA had the advantage that its instruments can be tested, evaluated, and, if necessary, replaced after every flight. The 747SP was operated from NASA's Armstrong Flight Research Center in Palmdale, California. Conversely, the Ames Research Center in Silicon Valley, California, coordinated the program inclusive of the scientific missions in cooperation with the American Universities Space Research Association and the German SOFIA Institute at the University of Stuttgart. The flying telescope was grounded for good in September 2022, as more inexepensive alternatives become available.

Opposite, above left: The centerpiece of SOFIA is its 22-ton, 8.9-foot telescope, made by High-Tech-Unternehmen of Germany, with an effective usable diameter of 8.2 feet. *NASA*

Opposite, below: Before the modification of the 747SP chosen to become SOFIA, the tricky conversion was tried out in the aft fuselage section of a scrapped 747SP with a full-scale model of the telescope. The experience gained then flowed into the conversion of the future flying Jumbo. *NASA*

Opposite, right: A schematic representation of the SOFIA cabin, with the workplaces for the research team in front and the telescope installed in the aft fuselage. *NASA*

Right: The 747SP is the third NASA jet used to carry an airborne telescope. The earlier telescopes were much smaller, however, and their performance was far inferior to that of SOFIA. *NASA*

Below: For its role as flying research laboratory, not only did the former passenger aircraft have to undergo considerable structural modification; it also had to be equipped with numerous additional systems for its global astronomical missions. *NASA*

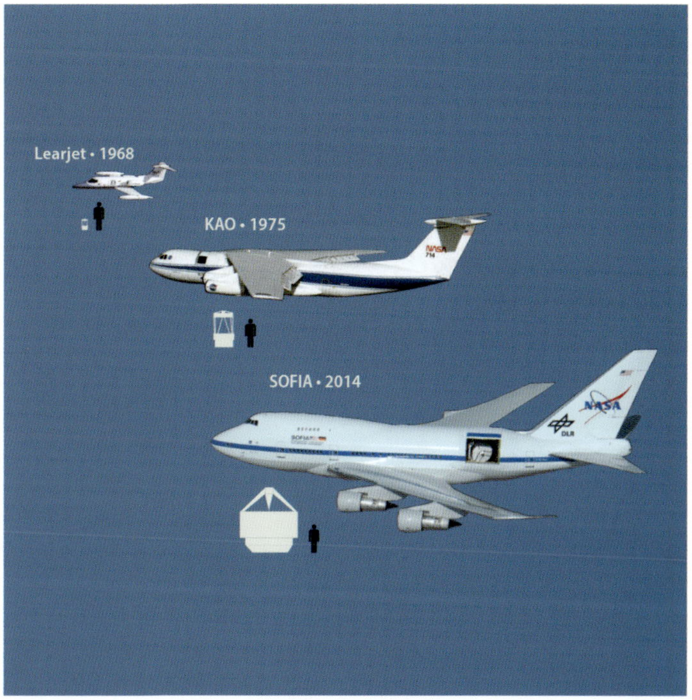

747 SCA: THE SPACE SHUTTLE CARRIER

At the beginning of the 1970s, NASA developed a transport system with whose help the reusable space shuttle could be transported back to the launch-and-landing complex at the Kennedy Space Center. With a length of 122 feet and a wingspan of 78 feet, the shuttle did not fit in any existing transport aircraft. Transport by land or sea was out of the question, since the distances to the alternate or emergency landing sites around the globe, which included the Cologne/Bonn airport, were too great. It seemed most practical to fly the shuttle to Florida mounted piggyback on an aircraft, for which the Boeing 747 was the most suitable American aircraft. NASA's Boeing 747 transports performed reliably from the first flight of the shuttle prototype *Enterprise*, which was not intended to go into space and was used for aerodynamic flight trials only, in September 1976, until the surviving space shuttles were consigned to museums after the *Endeavour* completed the last space mission on June 1, 2011. NASA acquired the first 747 destined to become a shuttle carrier aircraft from American Airlines in 1974. Before the 747-123, built in 1970, was modified for its new role, it served as a test aircraft to investigate the effects of dangerous wingtip vortices that trail from the wingtips of large aircraft such as the Boeing 747. These studies led the FAA to introduce new approach procedures with increased separation between light and heavy aircraft approaching commercial airports. After the tests had been completed, NASA 905 was finally modified for its actual mission at NASA's Dryden Flight Research Center. Since the second shuttle carrier, NASA 911, did not become available until 1990, NASA 905 flew the bulk of the shuttle transport missions, seventy of eighty-seven. These included forty-six of the fifty-four postmission ferry flights in which a shuttle was flown from the alternate landing site at Dryden back to the Kennedy Space Center. When the shuttle spaceflight ended, NASA 905 delivered the shuttles *Discovery*, *Enterprise*, and *Endeavour* to museums in Washington, DC; New York; and Los Angeles. After just 11,018 flight hours, including its time in service with American Airlines, NASA 905 was put on display at the Johnson Space Center in Houston, Texas. Transport missions by NASA 905 and its sister ship NASA 911 were coordinated from there. The latter was originally a 747-100SR-46 short-range version, which Boeing had built for Japan Air Lines to use on its domestic routes in 1973. After NASA acquired the 747 in 1989, Boeing converted it into an SCA and delivered the aircraft to NASA on November 20, 1990. By the time it was retired on February 8, 2012, NASA 911 had made 386 flights as a shuttle carrier aircraft—including a total of sixty-six carrying a space shuttle. This aircraft can be seen in the Joe Davies Heritage Airpark in Palmdale, California, not far from NASA's Dryden Flight Research Center.

Group photo of the crews of the Boeing 747 shuttle carrier aircraft and the shuttle prototype Enterprise in July 1977, after the conclusion of a series of flight tests. The tests included five takeoffs with the unpowered shuttle. In the process it separated from the mounting struts on top of the 747's fuselage at high altitude. *NASA*

In the course of space shuttle operations, NASA used two modified Boeing 747s to transport the vehicles. In this photo taken on August 19, 2005, the space shuttle Discovery is mounted on top of Shuttle Carrier Aircraft 905, flying from the NASA Flight Research Center in Dryden, California, across the American continent to the Kennedy Space Center in Florida. Discovery had landed in California from shuttle mission STS-114 ten days earlier. *NASA / Lori Losey*

BOEING 747-400LCF: THE DREAMLIFTER

When, in October 2003, Boeing announced that large components of its new long-range airliner would not be made in the region around Seattle, as was traditionally done, but would instead be produced by global suppliers in Asia and Europe, the project was still called the 7E7. Not until January 2005 did it officially become the 787 Dreamliner, whose intercontinental production chain would soon cause the Dreamliner to become a nightmare for Boeing. The complexity of the project and the resulting losses in quality and time delays were not, however, due to the transport system, for which Boeing—following the example of its European archrival Airbus—relies to this day on a converted type from its own house. There are now four Dreamlifters in service, which are officially called Large Cargo Freighters (LCF) by Boeing. The four converted Jumbos, which had previously served as passenger aircraft with Air China, China Airlines, and Malaysia Airlines, were likewise converted into transports for 787 components by an international program. Boeing's Moscow bureau helped design the LCF, as did the then subsidiary Boeing Rocketdyne, while the swing tail was designed by the Spanish development company Gamesa Aeronautica. The actual conversions were carried out in Taiwan by Evergreen Aviation Technologies Corporation. The first Dreamlifter rolled out of the assembly hangar on August 17, 2006, and on September 9 of that year it made a successful maiden flight from Taipei. The 747-400 LCF's appearance had little in common with the elegant look of all other 747 versions, and Scott Carson, then president of the Boeing civil aircraft division, apologized to Joe Sutter, who had conceived the Jumbo Jet in the 1960s, with the following words, which were probably not meant very seriously: "I'm sorry for what we've done to your aircraft." Flight testing of the voluminous Boeing freighter was carried out from Boeing's company airfield in the Seattle area, until on June 2, 2007, the type was issued its FAA certification. For operation of the fleet, which slowly grew to four aircraft, Boeing initially signed a contract with the American airfreight company Evergreen International Airlines; however, in August 2010 this was replaced by a ten-year contract with the freight carrier Atlas Air.

With its considerable width of 27.5 feet and a volume of 64,979 cubic feet, the 747-400 LCF's unpressurized cargo hold can even accommodate preassembled sections of the 18.9-foot 787 fuselage or wings and tail sections and fly them to Seattle for final assembly.

Boeing had previously modified passenger aircraft of Air China, China Airlines, and Malaysian Airlines into 747-400 Large Cargo Freighter (LCF). Dubbed the Dreamlifter, the modified Jumbos are needed for the global transport logistics of the Boeing 787. *Public domain*

Only the nose section is reminiscent of the once-elegant fuselage shape of the Boeing 747-400. *Public domain*

The Large Cargo Freighter design was created with the participation of the Moscow Boeing bureau as well as the then subsidiary Boeing Rocketdyne, while the folding tail was designed by the Spanish development company Gamesa Aeronautica. *Public domain*

747 SUPERTANKER: AERIAL FIREFIGHTER

Tanker 944 is the name of what was the largest firefighting aircraft in the world, based on a modified Boeing 747-400. The eight tanks in the aircraft, registered N744ST, could hold up to 19,205 US gallons of retardants in the form of water, powder, or foam, which could be dropped in a single pass over a 3-kilometer-long and approximately 164-foot-wide area or in up to six individual drops.

The American airfreight company Evergreen was the first to come up with the idea of converting Boeing 747s into firefighting aircraft. The reason behind it was two fatal crashes in the United States involving elderly Lockheed C-130 Hercules and Consolidated PB4Y-2 Privateer firefighting aircraft, whose modified structures were no longer equal to the loads imposed by their use as water bombers. The two aircraft had crashed within a space of two months during firefighting sorties, and in both cases the crashes resulted from the aircraft losing one or both wings. In order to protect the aircraft crews, in May 2004 the American Forestry Service announced that it was canceling contracts with operators of elderly firefighting aircraft, whereupon the Department of the Interior began looking for more-modern and safer alternatives—which led to the conversion of DC-10 and B747 wide-body jets for use as firefighting aircraft. Evergreen had equipped single examples of the 747-100 and -200 with a self-developed system, which enabled them to accurately distribute fire retardants stored in pressurized tanks over fires from a height of just 394 to 788 feet. During the drop phase the 747 flies with leading- and trailing-edge flaps extended at about 162 mph. Ensuring that the 747's center of gravity remains within limits when the water is dropped poses a particular challenge, and this is taken care of by a computer system patented by Evergreen. Evergreen received FAA certification for the complete tank installation in 2006. The first Supertanker, a converted 747-200 with the registration N470EV, took to the air for the first time on February 19, 2004. It was followed by the converted 747-100 with the registration N479EV. Both aircraft demonstrated their effectiveness while fighting forest fires in the United States, and in 2010 in Israel. But then Evergreen got into financial difficulties, which led to bankruptcy in 2013. The two Jumbo firefighters were initially flown to Pinal Park in the Arizona desert and there sold to a local aircraft recycler. In 2015, the newly founded company Global SuperTanker Services acquired the fully preserved Evergreen firefighting system, which was removed from the 747-100 and installed in a newer 747-400 with the registration N744ST. Included in the package in addition to the system hardware was the FAA certification for the fire-extinguishing system and a supply of spare parts plus the necessary documentation. Named Spirit of John Muir in memory of one of the first American conservationists, from its base in Colorado Springs the aircraft can reach anywhere in the United States within 4.5 hours, and fully fueled it has a radius of operation of 1,864 miles. In 2019, the Global SuperTanker helped fight fires in the Bolivian rainforest. The company ceased operations in April 2021, and the Supertanker was converted to a standard 747-400F freighter version destined for National Airlines.

The eight tanks of the largest firefighting aircraft in the world, registered N744ST, held up to 19,205 gallons of retardant in the form of water, powder, or foam. *Global Super Tanker Services, LLC*

The fire retardant carried by the modified Boeing 747-400 is sufficient to cover an area more than a kilometer long and about 50 meters wide in a single drop—or can be released in up to six individual drops. *Global Super Tanker Services, LLC*

US AIR FORCE E-4B: THE FLYING COMMAND POST

This special version of the 747-200 is operated by the US Air Force as a flying command post for use in the event of a nuclear attack. During the Cold War, one of the four E-4s that were built was manned twenty-four hours a day, so that the supreme commander could take off immediately in the event of a crisis. After relations between the United States and Russia became less strained, in 2007 consideration was given to retiring the small fleet; however, these original plans have been delayed ever since. The aircraft, which have been in service since 1974, are equipped with a multitude of channels of communication to the armed forces and, in the event of an emergency, make it possible for radio and television broadcasts to be made to the American people. The four aircraft, which are attached to the US Air Force's Air Combat Command, are also used to coordinate actions during natural catastrophes in the United States. In June 2017, a tornado damaged to E-4Bs parked at Offutt Air Force Base in the state of Nebraska. When this book went to print, no further information was available as to their future use.

Initially kept serviceable exclusively for use in the event of an attack on the United States, the E-4Bs have since also been used to coordinate operations during natural disasters in the United States. *US Air Force / TSgt. Jerry Morrison*

THE AUTHOR
WOLFGANG BORGMANN

Wolfgang Borgmann's enthusiasm for aviation was passed on to him by his parents, who were active in the aviation field. In his early years, he began building up an aviation historical collection that provides numerous rare photos and documents, as well as exciting background information, for his books. Since April 2000, Borgmann has been active as an author and freelance aviation journalist. Since February 2022, he has worked as editor for the leading German civil aviation magazine *Aero International.* He lives in Oerlinghausen, Germany. His website is www.aerojournalist.de.

SCHIFFER BOOKS *on Related Subjects*

SCHIFFER PUBLISHING

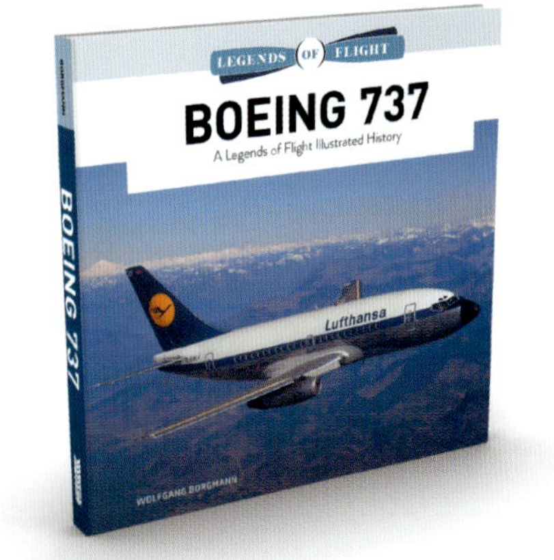

Boeing 737
A Legends of Flight Illustrated History
ISBN: 978-0-7643-6138-8 $29.99

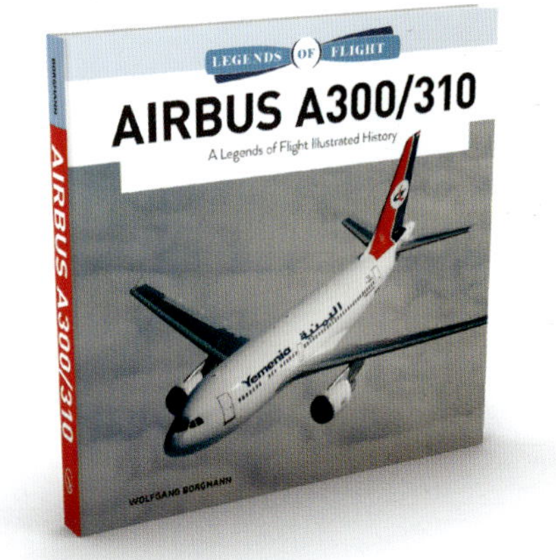

Airbus A300/310
A Legends of Flight Illustrated History
ISBN: 978-0-7643-6139-5 $29.99

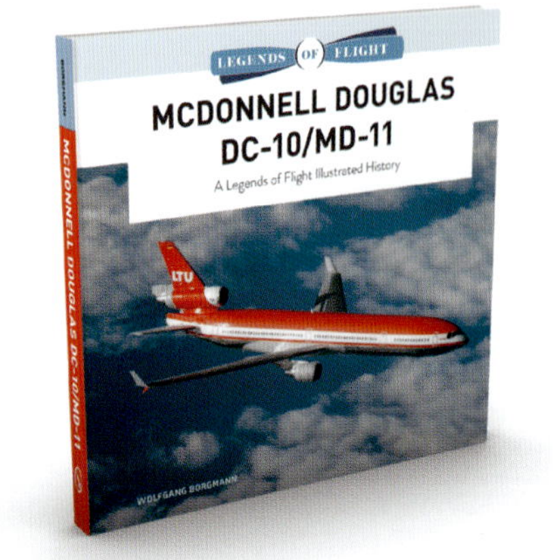

McDonnell DouglasDC-10/MD-11
A Legends of Flight Illustrated History
ISBN: 978-0-7643-6137-1 $$29.99

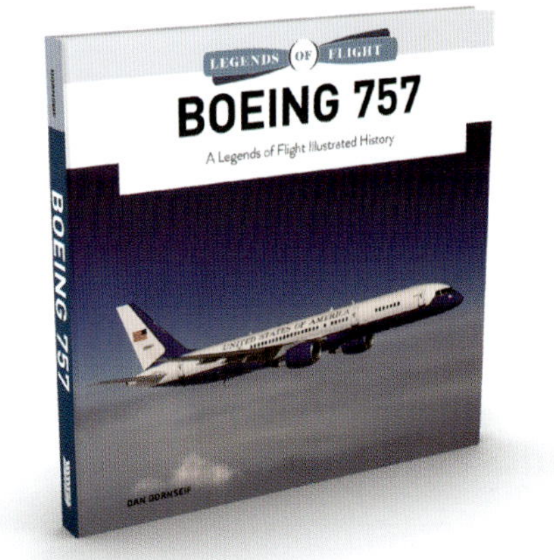

Boeing 757
A Legends of Flight Illustrated History
ISBN: 978-0-7643-6346-7 $29.99

747
BOEING 747-400
747
BOEING 747-500X
747